D1859492

RUDYARD KIPLING

RUDYARD KIPLING

A CRITICISM BY

RICHARD LE GALLIENNE

WITH A BIBLIOGRAPHY BY

JOHN LANE

GYAN

Published by

Gyan Publishing House
5, Ansari Road
Daryaganj, New Delhi-110002
Phone: 011-47034999, 9811692060
E-mail: books@gyanbooks.com

Distribution Network
gyanbooks.com
India, USA, Canada, UK, Australia, France

© Publisher

All rights reserved. No part of this work may be reproduced, stored, adapted, or transmitted in any form or by any means, electronic, mechanical, photocopying, micro-filming, recording or otherwise, or translated in any language, without the prior written permission of the copyright owner and the publisher.

ISBN : 978-81-212-9450-8 (PB)
First Published, 1900

2nd Impression 2023

Printed at: Gyan Press, Delhi.

The book is sold subject to the condition that it shall not, by way of trade or otherwise, be lent, resold, hired out, or otherwise circulated without the prior publisher's written consent.

RUDYARD KIPLING
Author: RICHARD LE GALLIENNE

RUDYARD KIPLING:

A CRITICISM

• RVDYARD • KIPLING •

RUDYARD KIPLING

A CRITICISM BY

RICHARD LE GALLIENNE

WITH A BIBLIOGRAPHY BY
JOHN LANE

"The fire-carriages shout the names of new gods that are *not* the old under new names. . . ."

"When Brahm cease to dream the heavens and the hells and earth disappear. Be content. Brahm dreams still."

The Bridge-Builders.

JOHN LANE: THE BODLEY HEAD
LONDON AND NEW YORK
1900

To

Helen Bartlett Bridgman

CONTENTS

NOTE

THE author acknowledges with thanks, permission to include extracts from the works of Mr. Kipling from Mr. Kipling himself, Mr. A. P. Watt, his agent, Messrs. Methuen & Co., Messrs. Macmillan & Co., Messrs. George Newnes, Ltd., Messrs. D. Appleton & Co., the Century Company, and the Doubleday McClure Company, his publishers in England and America; also to Messrs. Chatto and Windus, for similar permission in regard to Mr. Kipling's contribution to their publication, "My First Book."

RUDYARD KIPLING:

A CRITICISM

CHAPTER I

THE POETRY

1. *Introductory—" Departmental Ditties "*

The history of Mr. Rudyard Kipling's reputation, in this spring of 1899, lies between two phrases. In 1890 we were saying to each other, with a sense of freemasonry in a new cult: "But that is another story." To-day we are exhorting each other to: "Take up the white man's burden." The value of each phrase is about the value of Mr. Kipling's reputation in 1890 and 1899, respectively. The smart young Anglo-Indian story-teller is now a prophet. His fame is a church. Meanwhile, he has proved himself a poet such as no one could have foretold from those "Departmental Ditties" which made his introduction to English, as to Anglo-Indian, readers.

Considered merely abstractly, as one considers a meteor for its flight, the phenomena of Mr. Kipling's reputation are remarkable —the suddenness of his appearance, the decisiveness of it, and the speed of his publicity. In our day the reputation of Aubrey Beardsley is only more remarkable; for its instantaneousness, as by cable all round the world, was not, as in Mr. Kipling's case, the sudden spark of fame to a mine of work accumulated and already well known in another land—nor, need one say, was Beardsley gifted to be the darling of the Anglo-Saxon.

I have no sufficient data for considering Mr. Kipling's earlier Indian incarnation.

But I believe I am not wrong in thinking that the first man who said "Kipling" in an English journal was Sir William Hunter, the journal being *The Academy* (then edited by that enthusiastic Indian scholar, Mr. J. S. Cotton), and the occasion a review of "Departmental Ditties." The article impressed one rather by its prophetic note, than by the case Sir William Hunter was able to make out for quotations that seemed in themselves but little to prognosticate a great reputation. One gathered from the article that the young writer was already a person in India, and that his reputation was even then furiously on its way to us. So, indeed, it proved. Within a fortnight it had fallen upon us like a monsoon, and every paper one took up blew the beautiful shining trumpets of a fair young fame. Kipling was born.

If there had only been "Departmental Ditties" and "Plain Tales," things might not have gone so merrily. But Mr. Kipling had heavier metal in readiness to follow up this first attack, and almost immediately the book-stalls were stacked with green paper-backed pamphlets, looking shabby and weary as colonial books have a way of looking, bearing such titles as "Soldiers Three," "Under the Deodars," "Black and White," "The Story of the Gadsbys." Thus it was that all the work at the back of "Departmental Ditties," all the prodigious precocity of experience, told. It was when we read "the little green books" that we understood what Sir William Hunter meant.

Now "Departmental Ditties" was verse strictly "for those whom it might concern"; that is, for those whose lot was cast among the humours and chicaneries of Anglo-Indian officialdom. We can imagine them enjoying the hits hugely, as they read them week by week in various Indian papers. So do lawyers chuckle over the wicked little verses in *The Law Times*. The laughter which greets the "departmental" is necessarily limited in area, but it is proportionally hearty. And Mr. Kipling's first business was to win the laugh, or the tear, nearest to him.

The reader will remember the vivid picture of an Indian provincial newspaper office which occurs in "The Man who Would be King." As it was under the conditions there described that "Departmental Ditties" came into being, a quotation from that story will not be out of place:

"One Saturday night it was my pleasant duty to put the paper to bed alone. A King or courtier or a courtesan or a Community was going to die or get a new Constitution, or do something that was important on the other side of the world, and the paper was to be held open till the latest possible minute in order to catch the telegram.

It was a pitchy black night, as stifling

as a June night can be, and the *loo*, the red-hot wind from the westward, was booming among the tinder-dry trees and pretending that the rain was on its heels. Now and again a spot of almost boiling water would fall on the dust with the flop of a frog, but all our weary world knew that was only pretence. It was a shade cooler in the press-room than the office, so I sat there, while the type ticked and clicked, and the night-jars hooted at the windows, and the all but naked compositors wiped the sweat from their foreheads, and called for water. The thing that was keeping us back, whatever it was, would not come off, though the *loo* dropped and the last type was set, and the whole round earth stood still in the choking heat, with its finger on its lip, to wait the event. I drowsed, and wondered whether the telegraph was a blessing, and whether this dying man, or struggling people, might be aware of the inconvenience the delay was causing. There was no special reason beyond the heat and worry to make tension, but, as the clock-hands crept up to three o'clock, and the machines spun their fly-wheels two or three times to see that all was in order before I said the word that would set them off, I could have shrieked aloud."

To this it will be interesting to add something from Mr. Kipling's own account of the birth of his "little brown baby," contributed to *The Idler* a few years ago:

"As there is only one man in charge of a steamer, so there is but one man in charge of a newspaper, and he is the editor. My chief taught me this on an Indian journal, and he further explained that an order was an order, to be obeyed at a run, not a walk, and that any notion or notions as to the fitness or unfitness of any particular kind of work for the young had better be held over till the last page was locked up to press.

He was breaking me into harness, and I owe him a deep debt of gratitude, which I did not discharge at the time. The path of virtue was very steep, whereas the writing of verses allowed a certain play to the mind, and, unlike the filling in of reading matter, could be done as the spirit served. Now, a sub-editor is not hired to write verses: he is paid to sub-edit. At the time, this discovery shocked me greatly. . . . This is a digression, as all my verses were digressions from office work. They came without invitation, unmanneredly, in the nature of things; but they had to come, and the writing out of them kept me healthy and amused. To the best of my remembrance, no one then discovered their grievous cynicism, or their pessimistic tendency, and I was far too busy, and too happy, to take thought about these things. So they arrived merrily, being born out of the life about me, and they were very bad indeed, and the joy of doing them was payment a thousand times their worth. Some, of course, came and ran away again, and the dear sorrow of going in search of these (out of office hours, and catching them) was almost better than writing them clear. Bad as they were, I burned twice as many as were published, and of the survivors at least two-thirds were cut down at the last moment. Nothing can be wholly beautiful that is not useful, and therefore my verses were made to ease off the perpetual strife between the manager extending his advertisements and my chief fighting for his reading-matter. They were born to be sacrificed. Rukn-Din, the foreman of our side, approved of them immensely, for he was a Muslim of culture. He would say: 'Your potery very good, sir; just coming proper length to-day. You giving more soon? One-third column just proper. Always can take on third page. . . .' And in this manner, week by week, my verses came to be printed in the paper. I was in very good company, for there is always an undercurrent of song, a little bitter for the most part, running through the Indian papers. The bulk of it is much better than mine, being more graceful, and is done by those less than Sir Alfred Lyall—to whom I would apologise for mentioning his name in this gallery—'Pekin,' 'Latakia,' 'Cigarette,' 'O.,' 'T.W.,' 'Foresight,' and others, whose names come up with the stars out of the Indian Ocean going eastward.

Sometimes a man in Bangalore would be moved to song, and a man on the Bombay side would answer him, and a man in Bengal would echo back, till at last we would all be crowing together like cocks before daybreak, when it is too dark to see your fellow. And, occasionally, some unhappy Chaaszee, away in the China Ports, would lift up his voice among the tea-chests, and the queer-smelling yellow papers of the Far East brought us his sorrows. . . . My verses had the good fortune to last a little longer than some others, which were more true to facts and certainly better workmanship. Men in the Army, and the Civil Service, and the Railway, wrote to me saying that the rhymes might be made into a book. Some of them had been sung to the banjoes round campfires, and some had run as far down coast as Rangoon and Moulmein, and up to Mandalay. A real book was out of the question, but I knew that Rukn-Din and the office plant were at my disposal at a price, if I did not use the office time. Also, I had handled in the previous year a couple of small books, of which I was part owner, and had lost nothing. So there was built a sort of a book, a lean oblong docket, wire-stitched, to imitate a D. O. Government envelope, printed on one side only, bound in brown paper, and secured with red tape. It was addressed to all heads of departments and all Government officials, and among a pile of papers would have deceived a clerk of twenty years' service. Of these 'books' we made some hundreds, and as there was no necessity for advertising, my public being to my hand, I took reply-postcards, printed the news of the birth of the book on one side, the blank order-form on the other, and posted them up and down the Empire from Aden to Singapore, and from Quetta to Colombo. There was no trade discount, no reckoning twelves as thirteens, no commission, and no credit of any kind whatever. The money came back in poor but honest rupees, and was transferred from the publisher, the left-hand pocket, direct to the author, the right-hand pocket. Every copy sold in a few weeks, and the ratio of expenses to profits, as I remember it, has since prevented my injuring my health by sympathising with publishers who talk of their risks and advertisements. The down-country papers complained of the form of the thing. The wire binding cut the pages, and the red tape tore the covers. This was not intentional, but Heaven helps those who help themselves. Consequently, there arose a demand for a new edition, and this time I exchanged the pleasure of taking in money over the counter for that of seeing a real publisher's imprint on the title-page. More verses were taken out and put in, and some of that edition travelled as far as Hong Kong on the map, and each edition grew a little fatter, and, at last, the book came to London with a gilt top and a stiff back, and was advertised in the publishers' poetry department.

But I loved it best when it was a little brown baby with a pink string round its stomach; a child's child, ignorant that it was afflicted with all the most modern ailments; and before people had learned, beyond doubt, how its author lay awake of nights in India, plotting and scheming to write something that should 'take' with the English public."

This little brown baby is, very naturally,

one of the collector's treasures to-day, just as Mr. Kipling's first sock, or his first sailor-hat, would have its commercial value. Even a critic lingers thus unduly over his first book—if "Departmental Ditties" can be called a first book after the reference in the foregoing to "a couple of small books, of which I was part owner." What these books were I must leave the bibliographer to tell us.

From a literary, or any serious, point of view, indeed, "Departmental Ditties" are hardly more important than Mr. Kipling's first sailor-hat. That they should be scattered broadcast at sixpence is a little unfair to his position at the moment, though in many respects they are the very thing for a sixpenny public. For the most part they are sprightly imitations of American farcical verse-writers; the kind of knock-about poetry you find in comic recitation books—and often very funny poetry, too, in my humble opinion. For example, not specially of the funniness, but of the type—

> "Potiphar Gubbins, C.E.,
> Stands at the top of the tree;
> And I muse in my bed on the reasons that led
> To the hoisting of Potiphar G . . .
>
> Potiphar Gubbins, C.E.,
> Is coarse as a chimpanzee;
> And I can't understand why you gave him your hand,
> Lovely Mehitabel Lee."

'Boanerges Blitzen" and "Ahasuerus Jenkins" of the "Operatic Own" are two more names which give the *genre* better than many words—Anglo-Indian humours and ironies set to American farce-metres. For typical examples, and most amusing, read "The Post that Fitted" and "A Code of Morals." Then you have comic Poe to this tune:

"As I left the Halls at Lumley, rose the
vision of a comely
Maid last season worshipped dumbly,
watched with fervour from afar."

Comic Swinburne to this:

"Will you conquer my heart with your
beauty; my soul going out from afar?
Shall I fall to your hand as a victim of
crafty and cautious *shikar?*

Have I met you and passed you already,
unknowing, unthinking and blind?
Shall I meet you next session at Simla, oh
sweetest and best of your kind?"

Comic sentimental as thus:

"Open the old cigar-box, get me a Cuba
stout,
For things are running crossways, and Mag-
gie and I are out."

Comic Omar, too, applied to the dilemmas of the Indian budget:

"Now the New Year, reviving last Year's
Debt,
The thoughtful Fisher casteth wide his
Net;
So I with begging Dish and ready Tongue
Assail all Men for all that I can get."

You will find, also, a comic "ballade," duly furnished with an envoi beginning "Princess."

Personally, I like Mr. Kipling for beginning with the "bones." It was a healthy sign. And here and there amid all the imitative patter there were struck notes, somewhat deeper, which we can recognise now for signs of what was to come. In "Pagett, M.P." we first hear his impatience with the dilettante grandees who make their fair-weather studies of the East, and pooh-pooh the hard lot of the Anglo-Indian official. Pagett didn't believe in the stories of Indian heat, till April with its sandflies, May with its dust-storms, June with its dysentery, and July with its "Cholera Morbus," convinced him, and he returned home:

"And I laughed as I drove from the station, but the mirth died out on my lips
As I thought of the fools like Pagett who write of their 'Eastern trips,'
And the sneers of the travelled idiots who duly misgovern the land,
And I prayed to the Lord to deliver another one into my hand."

Then there was the ballad of Jack Barrett, who was sent to Quetta for official reasons worth quoting at length:

"Jack Barrett went to Quetta
Because they told him to.
He left his wife at Simla
On three-fourths his monthly screw.

Jack Barrett died at Quetta
  Ere the next month's pay he drew.

. . .

Jack Barrett went to Quetta
  And there gave up the ghost·
Attempting two men's duty
  In that very healthy post;
And Mrs. Barrett mourned for him
  Five lively months at most.

Jack Barrett's bones at Quetta
  Enjoy profound repose;
But I shouldn't be astonished
  If *now* his spirit knows
The reason of his transfer
  From the Himalayan snows.

And, when the Last Great Bugle Call
  Adown the Hurnai throbs,
When the last grim joke is entered
  In the big black Book of Jobs,

And Quetta graveyards give again
  Their victims to the air,
I shouldn't like to be the man
  Who sent Jack Barrett there."

And there were two sea-ballads: "The Ballad of Fisher's Boarding-House," and "The Galley Slave" particularly which secreted hints of the brutal vigour and knock-down metaphor of "The Ballad of the 'Bolivar.'" There were also early spring shoots of Mr. Kipling's aphoristic gift: for example—

"The toad beneath the harrow knows
Exactly where each tooth-point goes,
The butterfly upon the road
Preaches contentment to that toad."

And—

"If She have spoken a word, remember thy
  lips are sealed,
And the Brand of the Dog is upon him by
  whom is the secret revealed.

If She have written a letter, delay not an
instant but burn it.
Tear it in pieces, O Fool, and the wind to
her mate shall return it!
If there be trouble to Herward, and a lie of
the blackest can clear,
Lie, while thy lips can move or a man is
alive to hear."

In spite of the chivalry of the last quotation, there were hints not uncertain of Mr. Kipling's general, amused, somewhat contemptuous and bitter, and entirely fatherly, view of women:

"For Maggie has written a letter to give
me my choice between
The wee little whimpering Love and the
great god Nick o' Teen."

That was the trouble referred to in an earlier quotation. The surface moral of the story is that no true man could think twice before choosing—the cigar; but, of course, the real moral, if I am not taking a triviality too seriously, is that a woman worth having wouldn't make such a silly condition. It is the old story of the lady who threw her glove down among the lions, and received it back in her face. Women are not like that quite always in Mr. Kipling's writings.

To make an end with "Departmental Ditties," one may further instance a prologue and an epilogue, striking a note of artistic seriousness which the intermediate pages hardly support; as though a nigger-minstrel with banjo and blackened face should whisper that he is M. Paderewski in disguise; a note of beauty and pathos, too:

"For it may be, if still we sing
And tend the Shrine,
Some Deity on wandering wing
May here incline;
And, finding all in order meet,
Stay while we worship at Her feet."

That deity was to visit the shrine in another volume. Meanwhile, "Departmental Ditties," to one looking forward, could have little significance; but to us, looking backward, we can see that Mr. Kipling was already tuning his banjo to such purpose that it might even, on occasion, do duty as a lyre.

2. "*Barrack-Room Ballads.*"

Mr. Kipling has followed the pleasant old fashion, chiefly associated with Scott, of giving his stories a verse motto usually written by himself. Often in "Plain Tales" these verses struck one more than the tales themselves. There had been nothing in "Departmental Ditties" so good as:

"Go, stalk the red deer o'er the heather,
Ride, follow the fox if you can!
But, for pleasure and profit together,
Allow me the hunting of Man,—

The chase of the Human, the search for the Soul
To its ruin,—the hunting of Man."

Or this:

"Wherefore slew you the stranger? He brought me dishonour.
I saddled my mare Bijli. I set him upon her.
I gave him rice and goat's flesh. He bared me to laughter;
When he was gone from my tent, swift I followed after,
Taking a sword in my hand. The hot wine had filled him:
Under the stars he mocked me. Therefore I killed him."

Or, in another vein, this:

"In the daytime, when she moved about me,
In the night, when she was sleeping at my side,—

I was wearied, I was wearied of her presence,
Day by day and night by night I grew to hate her—
Would God that she or I had died."

Or this:

"Not though you die to-night, O Sweet, and wail,
A spectre at my door,
Should mortal Fear make Love immortal fail—
I shall but love you more,
Who, from Death's house returning, give me still
One moment's comfort in my matchless ill."

Then there was this of "Little Tin Gods":

"Pleasant it is for the Little Tin Gods
When great Jove nods;

But Little Tin Gods make their little mistakes
In missing the hour when great Jove wakes";

and the longer mystical poem in front of "To be Filed for Reference." But, perhaps, more than by any of these one's fancy had been caught by a few snatches in Cockney dialect labelled "Barrack-Room Ballad," and particularly this:

"Oh! Where would I be when my froat was dry?
Oh! Where would I be when the bullets fly?
Oh! Where would I be when I come to die?
Why,
Somewheres anigh my chum.
If 'e's liquor 'e'll give me some,
If I'm dyin' 'e'll 'old my 'ead,
An' 'e'll write 'em 'Ome when I'm dead.—
Gawd send us a trusty chum!"

We hoped for more like that, and we had not long to wait. Presently the news went round that Mr. Kipling was contributing some quite fascinating ballads to *The Scots Observer*, a weekly journal, since defunct, edited with sword and pen by Mr. W. E. Henley; and, long before the volume entitled "Barrack-Room Ballads" appeared, "Danny Deever," "Fuzzy-Wuzzy," and "Mandalay" had become household words. There was a go and a catchiness about them that no English ballads had possessed since Macaulay. When the volume appeared it was more widely read than any poetry published for some years. It was that rare thing in poetry, a genuinely popular success; and the success was significant of the achievement.

By that volume Mr. Kipling as a poet must still be judged. It contained poems which he has certainly not surpassed since, if, indeed, he has equalled them, and it revealed limitations which he has not yet surmounted. In few volumes has the cleavage between what a man can do and what he can not do been so marked. And, with one or two exceptions presently to be noted, the cleavage was between the "Barrack-Room Ballads" and the "Other Verses." Re-reading the volume again to-day, one returns to one's first conclusion. The best of the "Barrack-Room Ballads" still retain their magic, but the "Other Verses" still leave one cold, and, to be frank, a little bored.

Of the ballad, or rather of one kind of ballad, Mr. Kipling is clearly a master; that is the singing ballad, with swinging jingle choruses and catchy refrains, *and* written in dialect; but not the narrative ballad written in simple English. Nor, broadly speaking, can he write any kind of poetry in simple English. As a poet he stands or falls with dialect. Any minor qualifications this statement may seem to need will be made in due course. Our concern, for the moment, is with the "Barrack-Room Ballads."

These are not, of course, of equal excellence. Out of twenty-one there are, perhaps, not more than seven that one cares about reading again, but these seven are "Mandalay," "Danny Deever," "Fuzzy-Wuzzy," "Tommy," "Oonts," "Gunga Din," and "Soldier, Soldier." Of these the first four are, in their several ways, perfect things. The delicious humour, the biting irony, and the irresistible music-hall swing of "Fuzzy-Wuzzy" and "Tommy"; the tragic shiver and mournful music of "Danny Deever"; the romance and melody and passion of "Mandalay."

Here again in poetry was something that made us unspeakably glad. You might rank them this high or that, but without doubt they were real things, perfect things of their kind; in their degree as satisfactory as "Kubla Khan," or a number from

"The Mikado," or a song by Mr. Albert Chevalier. They were, indeed, as Orphic in their possession of us as "Knocked 'em in the Old Kent Road," or "Ta-ra-ra-boom-de-ay"; but, unlike those fascinating masterpieces, they were not dependent upon histrionic or musical interpretation. They won us by sheer literary effect. You had but to read them, and they provided their own dance-music. They lose, in my opinion, by being set to music—which is one of the signs of their being real poetry. Real poetry can as seldom be "set" as it can be illustrated. Also, one is struck, particularly in "Mandalay," with Mr. Kipling's wonderful transmuting use of the commonest material. Its magic is made of the very refuse of language. It reminds one of the magic of certain paintings, say a portrait by Mr. Sargent, which, close at hand, looks all slaps and dashes of paint, like an untidy palette; but, as we move further and further away, the vision comes out of the chaos, and soon we forget the brush-marks in the beauty. Similarly with the best of these "Barrack-Room Ballads," the poor Cockneyisms are transfigured out of recognition by imagination working at white heat, and a rhythm that might set rocks to dance-music. And could love-poetry be tenderer than:

"'Er petticoat was yaller an' 'er little cap was green,
An' 'er name was Supi-yaw-lat—jes' the same as Theebaw's Queen,
An' I seed her first a-smokin' of a whackin' white cheroot,
An' a-wastin' Christian kisses on an 'eathen idol's foot:
Bloomin' idol made o' mud—
Wot they called the Great Gawd Budd—
Plucky lot she cared for idols when I kissed 'er where she stud!
On the road to Mandalay. . . ."

Never is the miracle of art more fully brought home to us than when such coarse material is thus touched to finer issues. There is a piquant beauty, coming, of course, of the meeting of extremes in form and material, about a modelling in clay that, perhaps, hardly survives in the marble: though this observation suggests another. It reminds us that clay is perishable.

The other fourteen "Barrack-Room Ballads" have, of course, their interest, their humours, and their good lines; but that interest is mainly technical. They contribute their share to Mr. Kipling's picture of the British soldier in India, but their value stops there. They are not universalised, as work that remains with us must be. No doubt "that strong man T. A." (to whom Mr. Kipling dedicated "Soldiers Three") might rejoice in them were they published within his reach, just in the same way as Anglo-Indian Civil servants may still chuckle over "Departmental Ditties"; but they might as well be the slang ditties of Roman soldiers at the siege of Carthage for all their general, and anything like permanent, significance.

To consider now the "Other Verses." These, I said before, are mainly interesting as showing what Mr. Kipling can not do. But I referred to one or two exceptions. Of these much the most important is "The Ballad of the 'Bolivar,'" which is of the same *genre* as the "Barrack-Room Ballads." Mr. Kipling has written more ambitious sea-ballads, but this is easily first. It is marred by the inartistic use of technical terms incomprehensible to any but the nautical reader, but its imaginative vitality is such, its metaphor is so simply forcible, its rhythm so compelling, that they overcome all its flaws, and fix it securely in the memory.

With less emphasis I would except also the nautical "L'Envoi":

"There's a whisper down the field where
the year has shot her yield,
And the ricks stand grey to the sun,
Singing:—'Over then, come over, for the
bee has quit the clover,
And your English summer's done.'
You have heard the beat of the off-
shore wind,
And the thresh of the deep-sea
rain;
You have heard the song—how long!
how long?
Pull out on the trail again! . . .

Fly forward, O my heart, from the Fore-
land to the Start—
We're steaming all too slow,
And it's twenty thousand mile to our little
lazy isle
Where the trumpet-orchids blow!
You have heard the call of the off-
shore wind,
And the voice of the deep-sea rain;

You have heard the song—how long! how long?
Pull out on the trail again!

Two more exceptions I would make—poems of a different nature: "The Conundrum of the Workshops" and "Tomlinson." For satire in verse Mr. Kipling has a marked gift. He hits as hard as Tennyson could do now and again when he was so minded, though his method is rougher and more diffuse. The method of "Tomlinson," so far as its metre and rough-and-ready imagination go, Mr. Kipling learnt, I think, from Mr. Buchanan in such ballads as "The Vision of the Man Accurst." Using it thus, humorously, Mr. Kipling achieves his end of introducing "Tomlinson"; that is, of fixing in caricature a type not before pinned down. Tomlinson now stands for one of those book-fed, half-and-half dilettante products of civilisation, who have never really lived at all, never done good enough to take them to heaven, or evil enough to gain them admission into hell:

" 'This I have read in a book,' he said,
'and that was told to me,
And this I have thought that another man
thought of a Prince in Muscovy.' "

Tomlinson, as the phrase is, has passed into the language; at all events, into current mythology. But, once having been introduced to him, we have no further desire to read his letter of introduction. The method is just a little common even for satire. Only the force of the idea saves it. Tomlinson steps out of the verses, as a chicken out of its shell—and we think no more of the shell. The method is what one might call Mr. Kipling's "cosmic" method. For purposes of satire it is very effective; but to see into what disaster it may lead, one must read (to refer back a moment) the poem in which Mr. Kipling dedicates his ballads to the memory of his brother-in-law, Wolcott Balestier. The poem is too long to quote entire, but a verse or two will suffice:

"Beyond the path of the outmost sun through utter darkness hurled—
Further than ever comet flared or vagrant star-dust swirled—
Live such as fought and sailed and ruled and loved and made our world. . . .

'Tis theirs to sweep through the ringing deep where Azrael's outposts are,
Or buffet a path through the Pit's red wrath when God goes out to war,
Or hang with the reckless Seraphim on the rein of a red-maned star. . . .

And ofttimes cometh our wise Lord God, master of every trade,
And tells them tales of His daily toil, of Edens newly made;
And they rise to their feet as He passes by, gentlemen unafraid.

The big hyperboles with which Mr. Kipling here tries to bridge time and space suggest a too conscious stretching of the octave, and the large colloquialisms in which he presents the heavenly powers utterly fail in dignity. Nor is the impressiveness of the poem for its special purpose increased for old readers of *The Scots Observer*, by their remembering that a great part of it had already done duty as a satire *à propos* a notorious London exhibition of Rabelais pictures.

But this is by the way. There remains to speak of "The Conundrum of the Workshops"; from a literary point of view a more piquant performance than "Tomlinson." Mr. Kipling is fond of sneering at "Art with a big A." Evidently he had been, very naturally, nauseated with the cant talk about "Art," which, like his hero, "Dick Heldar," he found current in London. No doubt certain criticisms on his work provoked his bitter, witty rejoinder. All the same, Mr. Kipling knows well enough that, however you spell it, there is a form of lasting creation with pen and ink, with brushes and paint, with marble and chisel, and with musical notes, which we call "art," which also has its eternal laws not to be set aside for any of us, not even for Mr. Kipling; and that this art is not stultified of her foolish children, however foolish their talk.

Mr. Kipling represents the devil as the arch-critic. Whatever man has done he has always been there to cry: "You did it, but was it Art?" On the whole, a very proper question to ask—of the artist. Adam, and Noah, and the builders of Babel, were not artists, but strong men of action. The question was irrelevant to them. Mr. Kipling chose his examples badly for the force of his satire. Only in the last verse but one is the example to the point:

"When the flicker of London sun falls
faint on the Club-room's green and
gold,

The sons of Adam sit them down and
scratch with their pens in the mould—
They scratch with their pens in the mould
of their graves, and the ink and the
anguish start,
For the Devil mutters behind the leaves:
'It's pretty, but is it Art?'"

Of course. And only by steadily asking this question of contemporary reputations, as they blaze up on the horizon, can one hope to maintain a standard of serious work. Of course, if by art one means sugar-candy and stained-glass windows, it is another matter. But those who speak of art in its proper sense are not to be mocked out of their use of the only word for their purpose by satire, however telling, against those who take that word in vain.

I hope Mr. Kipling will overlook my saying it—but "Mandalay" is something very like *Art!* It's "human," it's "striking," it's "clever," it's "pretty," Mr. Kipling "did it"—and yet, it is *Art!*

Yes, and as sure as "Mandalay" is "art," something like seventeen poems included in the "Other Verses" are not. For eleven of these no one whose opinion counts could seriously plead. "The Last Suttee," "The Ballad of the King's Mercy," "The Ballad of the King's Jest," "With Scindia to Delhi," "The Lament of the Border Cattle Thief," "The Ballad of the 'Clampherdown,'" "The Sacrifice of Er-Heb," "The Explanation," "The Gift of the Sea," "Evarra and his Gods," "The Legend of Evil," are all commonplace, dull, or bad, in their several ways. "The Ballad of Boh Da Thone" is cheap burlesque that might have passed in "Departmental Ditties"; and "Cleared" and "An Imperial Rescript" are satires wrong-headedly conceived and indifferently executed.

Three poems only remain: "The Ballad of East and West," "The Rhyme of the Three Captains," and "The English Flag." I am aware that these poems have been highly praised. "The English Flag" begins well. Its first eight lines are spirited. They stir one. Were the rest of the poem equal to them, the poem had been a success. But they are not. Recondite geography—Mr. Kipling's fatal geography—and astronomy, are called in to take the place of inspiration; and, as nothing can take its place, they fail. "The Ballad of East and West" is generally better, though not so good in any single passage. It tells a stirring story stirringly, but the Macaulay-ish method of its telling is outworn. We can suffer ballads that go like this no more—the metre is worn out:

"Kamal is out with twenty men to raise the Border-side,
And he has lifted the Colonel's mare that is the Colonel's pride:
He has lifted her out of the stable-door between the dawn and the day,
And turned the calkins upon her feet, and ridden her far away."

As for "The Rhyme of the Three Captains," I may be at fault, for I have never been able to read it to the end; but so far as I have gone its story struck me as dull, its nautical technicalities, choking it like sea-weed, more than usually tiresome, and its metre open to the same objection as that brought against "The Ballad of East and West."

I have called eleven of Mr. Kipling's poems commonplace, dull, or bad. The statement, I am aware, is sweeping; yet considerations of space prevent my supporting my opinion with more than two or three quotations. Dulness is a pervasive quality difficult to illustrate in small samples. Yet one may fairly guess that a poem which begins as begins "The Ballad of the King's Jest" is going to be as dull all through. The lifeless beat of the couplet alone settles it. The most brilliant poetic idea could not keep itself awake in company with so somnolent a metre. Here are the opening lines:

"When spring-time flushes the desert grass,
Our kafilas wind through the Khyber Pass.
Lean are the camels but fat the frails,
Light are the purses but heavy the bales,
And the snowbound trade of the North
comes down
To the market-square of Peshawur town.

In a turquoise twilight, crisp and chill,
A kafila camped at the foot of the hill.
Then blue smoke-haze of the cooking
rose,
And tent-peg answered to hammer nose;
And the picketed ponies, shag and wild,
Strained at their ropes as the feed was
piled. . . ."

This is what I call dull poetry, and I think it may serve as an illustration of what I mean by bad poetry, too. This also is what Mr. Kipling makes of the couplet.

Here is an example of his blank verse from "The Sacrifice of Er-Heb":

"This is Taman, the God of all Er-Heb,
Who was before all Gods, and made all
Gods,
And presently will break the Gods he made,
And step upon the Earth to govern men
Who give him milk-dry ewes and cheat his
Priests,
Or leave his shrine unlighted—as Er-Heb
Left it unlighted and forgot Taman,
When all the Valley followed after Kysh
And Yabosh, little Gods but very wise,
And from the sky Taman beheld their sin."

Perhaps this might serve as an example of dulness, too.

"The Ballad of the 'Clampherdown'" and "The Lament of the Border Cattle Thief" are examples of what Mr. Kipling can do with the more conventional forms of ballad metre. Here is a verse from the first:

"It was our war-ship 'Clampherdown'
Would sweep the Channel clean,

Wherefore she kept her hatches close
When the merry Channel chops arose,
To save the bleached marine."

And here a verse from the second:

"O woe is me for the merry life
I led beyond the Bar,
And a treble woe for my winsome wife
That weeps at Shalimar."

It is largely the fault of Mr. Kipling's own achievement if such verse seems tame after "The 'Bolivar.'" But the simple truth is that Burns was not more de-poetized, cramped, and conscious, when he left his native Scotch to write Thomsonian English, than Mr. Kipling when he forsakes his inspiring Cockney—or at all events, some form of dialect. And this we shall find no less true of his second volume, "The Seven Seas," which we have now to consider.

3. "*The Seven Seas.*"

Still, the general average of "The Seven Seas" is higher than the general average of "Barrack-Room Ballads"; or, perhaps one should say, that the proportion of good second-class poems is larger. In fact, there is hardly a poem in the volume that has not some redeeming merit, of feeling or phrase. And if there is no "Mandalay," there is at least one poem supreme beyond the others, the pitiful ballad, "Mary, Pity Women." Here once more Mr. Kipling takes the very mud and orange-peel of the gutter, with an honest disregard of squeamish stomachs, and makes a symbol of tragedy and pity, which I shall leave "the Master of All Good Workmen," whom he invokes in his envoi, to praise.

"Mary, Pity Women," obviously belongs to the barrack-room section of the volume, and with the poems in that section we may as well deal before turning to the sea-poems. They well keep up the average of the first volume. In fact, rank and file, I think they are better. But there's no "Fuzzy-Wuzzy" or "Danny Deever." As near as we approach the latter is in "Cholera Camp," with its almost unbearably mournful refrain:

"*Oh, strike your camp an' go, the bugle's callin',*
The Rains are fallin'—
The dead are hushed an' stoned to keep 'em safe below;
The Band's a-doin' all she knows to cheer us;
The chaplain's gone and prayed to Gawd to 'ear us—
To 'ear us—
O Lord, for it's a killin' of us so!"

But the strength of this second instalment is in their humour, in the delightful devil-may-care fun of "The Shut-Eye Sentry" and "The Jacket":

"So it was 'Rounds! What rounds?' at two of a frosty night,
'E's 'oldin' on by the sergeant's sash, but, sentry, shut your eye.
An' it was 'Pass! All's well!' Oh, ain't 'e drippin' tight!
'E'll need an affidavit pretty badly by-an'-by"—

in the Mulvaney spirit of "The Men that Fought at Minden," a ballad of the breaking-in of poor young "recruities"; in the delightful frankness of "The Ladies," "An' I learned about women from 'er"; and in the quaint phrases of "Soldier an' Sailor Too"—"'E's a kind of a giddy harum-frodite—soldier an' sailor too!" But, perhaps, better than any of the ballads (except, of course, "Mary, Pity Women") is Mr. Kipling's charming prologue in regard to his "art":

> "*When 'Omer smote 'is bloomin' lyre,*
> *He'd 'eard men sing by land an' sea;*
> *An' what he thought 'e might require,*
> *'E went an' took—the same as me!*"

Turning to "The Seven Seas" section, one remarks that Mr. Kipling is growing more ambitious, also that his songs of the sea do not seem to come so natural to him as his soldier songs. There is more evidence of the determined note-book. Soldiers he learnt in the receptive, comparatively unconscious, period of boyhood; sailors he has had to cram. The same applies to his sea-stories, as I shall have further occasion to note later on.

Two ambitions firmly define themselves in "The Seven Seas": to sing the song of the Empire, and to sing the song of steam;

to unite our scattered colonies in a song, and, like Whitman, "in the labours of engines and the fields, to show the developments and the eternal meanings." From a literary point of view Mr. Kipling has succeeded best with steam, though in both cases he brings evidences of energetic intention rather than achievement. Still a persistent sentiment goes a long way, makes up for a good deal, in poetry, and when one's theme is so popular as the British Empire, the Empire itself is likely to help us out with the chorus.

Only as the work of the author of "Barrack-Room Ballads," and the story-teller of Anglo-India, could that mild cantata, "A Song of the English," have any significance; though in its opening number, "Fair is our lot, O goodly is our heritage," it sounds the first note of Mr. Kipling's later Methodistical-jingoistic manner. Never, throughout all its metrical devices, does it once catch fire; and the idea of Bombay,

Calcutta, Madras, and a dozen other cities and colonies, singing four lines apiece, like the lifeless personifications of the old masques, was one which no poet could carry out successfully. In the "Hymn before Action" we approach still nearer to the "Recessional" spirit:

> "The earth is full of anger,
>   The seas are dark with wrath,
> The Nations in their harness
>   Go up against our path:
> Ere yet we loose the legions—
>   Ere yet we draw the blade,
> Jehovah of the Thunders,
>   Lord God of Battles, aid!"

but as yet it is imperialism without the inflammatory jingle, so no one remarks it. In fact, among the serious poems of "The Seven Seas" section there are only two that can be said to stand out: "M'Andrews' Hymn" and "The Mary Gloster"; and, though it has found fewer to praise it, "The Mary Gloster" is much the superior of the two. "M'Andrews' Hymn" is interesting mainly for its intention—"to sing the Song o' Steam." The old Scotch engineer, with his Calvinism; his, so to say, sincere Scotch hypocrisy; his hinted humanity "at Gay Street in Hong Kong"; and his one real passion in life for his "seven thousand horse-power," is not so alive as his fellow in prose—McPhee of "Bread Upon the Waters"—and he would be distinctly tiresome but for some good lines Mr. Kipling puts into his mouth:

"That minds me of our Viscount loon—
  Sir Kenneth's kin—the chap
Wi' Russia leather tennis-shoon an' spar-
  decked yachtin' cap.
I showed him round last week, o'er all—
  an' at the last says he:
'Mister M'Andrews, don't you think steam
  spoils romance at sea?'

Damned ijjit! I'd been doon that morn to see what ailed the throws,
Manholin', on my back—the cranks three inches off my nose.
Romance! Those first-class passengers they like it very well,
Printed an' bound in little books; but why don't poets tell?
I'm sick of all their quirks an' turns—the loves an' doves they dream—
Lord, send a man like Robbie Burns to sing the Song o' Steam!
To match wi' Scotia's noblest speech yon orchestra sublime
Whaurto—uplifted like the Just—the tail-rods mark the time.

The crank-throws give the double-bass, the feed-pump sobs an' heaves,
An' now the main eccentrics start their quarrel on the sheaves:
Her time, her own appointed time, the rocking link-head bides,

Till—hear that note?—the rod's return
 whings glimmerin' through the guides.
They're all awa! True beat, full power,
 the clangin' chorus goes
Clear to the tunnel where they sit, my purrin' dynamoes.
Interdependence absolute, foreseen, ordained, decreed,
To work, ye'll note, at any tilt an' every
 rate o' speed.
Fra skylight-lift to furnace-bars, backed,
 bolted, braced an' stayed,
An' singin' like the Mornin' Stars for joy
 that they are made;
While, out o' touch o' vanity, the sweatin'
 thrust-block says:
'Not unto us the praise, or man—not unto
 us the praise!'"

Surely this last line is a little too much—even for an old Scotch humbug like M'Andrew. However, the poem is an interesting "intention." It is not quite the "Abt

Vogler" of steam—now Browning could have taught Mr. Kipling something about the use, and abuse, of technicalities in poetry—but it is something towards it.

In "The Mary Gloster," however, in spite of its Clement Scottish—or should it be G. R. Simsian—metre, we have a piece of characterisation such as Mr. Kipling seldom achieves. An old parvenu ship-owner, dying a "baronite"; but, for all his title and wealth, still the rough old pagan skipper, who has made a fortune by dint of sailing anything that was given him. He had been backed up by a plucky, little, ambitious wife, and she, though buried long since, is to the end, in spite of frankly confessed infidelities of no account, the ruling spirit of his life. Such is Sir Anthony Gloster, as he lies on his death-bed and damns his dilettante Harrow and Oxford son, with delightful and instructive candour. His last desire is to be taken out in the old "Mary Gloster" and buried at sea in the exact spot where his wife was buried, and he offers his son five thousand pounds to take him there. Mr. Kipling has seldom done better than in the old man's last wandering speech, a remarkably outspoken statement of the whole morality of man:

"Mary, why didn't *you* warn me? I've
 allus heeded to you,
Excep'—I know—about women; but you
 are a spirit now;
An', wife, they was only women, and I was
 a man. That's how.
An' a man 'e must go with a woman, as
 you could not understand;
But I never talked 'em secrets. I paid 'em
 out o' hand.
Thank Gawd, I can pay for my fancies!
 Now what's five thousand to me,
For a berth off the Paternosters in the haven
 where I would be?
I believe in the Resurrection, if I read my
 Bible plain,

But I wouldn't trust 'em at Wokin'; we're
    safer at sea again.
For the heart it shall go with the treasure—
    go down to the sea in ships.
I'm sick of the hired women—I'll kiss my
    girl on her lips!
I'll be content with my fountain, I'll drink
    from my own well,
And the wife of my youth shall charm me
    —an' the rest can go to Hell!"

"The Rhyme of the Three Sealers" must share the condemnation of "The Rhyme of the Three Captains" and "The Ballad of East and West," though it is better than either. Of the definitely nautical songs, the Anchor Song (from "Many Inventions"), in spite of its merciless technicalities, succeeds by the curiously blended sadness and gladness of its music—sadness of farewell, gladness of putting out to sea. But, perhaps, the most catchy of all the sea-songs is one which doesn't pretend to be a sea-song at all, but only a lament for the extinction of the three-volume novel, symbolised as "The Three-Decker." The more modern novel is symbolised as a modern steamer, and it will be seen that Mr. Kipling, in pursuit of his image, is obliged, for the moment, to go back on M'Andrew:

"That route is barred to steamers: you'll
never lift again
Our purple-painted headlands or the lordly
keeps of Spain.
They're just beyond your skyline, howe'er
so far you cruise
In a ram-you-damn-you liner with a brace
of bucking screws.

Swing round your aching search-light—
'twill show no haven's peace.
Ay, blow your shrieking sirens to the deaf,
grey-bearded seas!
Boom out the dripping oil-bags to skin the
deep's unrest—

And you aren't one knot the nearer to the
Islands of the Blest!

Here in this casual, accidental way, perhaps Mr. Kipling has caught more of

"The beauty and mystery of the ships
And the magic of the sea"

than in any of his more determined sea-ballads. "The Story of Ung," and "In the Neolithic Age"—the latter with its refrain

"There are nine and sixty ways of constructing tribal lays,
And-every-single-one-of-them-is-right"—

may be added to "The Conundrum of the Workshops" as good examples of Mr. Kipling's *jeux d'ésprit* on the subject of "art"; and to these may be added two poems *à propos* romance: one the obscure hymn "To the True Romance" (from

"Many Inventions"), and the other entitled "The King," and containing the whole matter in a line-and-a-half:

> "And all unseen
> Romance brought up the nine-fifteen."

I must not forget the "Sestina of the Tramp Royal," which embodies in a humourous epilogue the restless sailor spirit of wandering that breathes through the whole book:

> "Therefore, from job to job I've moved along.
> Pay couldn't 'old me when my time was done,
> For something in my 'ead upset me all,
> Till I 'ad dropped whatever 'twas for good,
> An', out at sea, be'eld the dock-lights die,
> An' met my mate—the wind that tramps the world!

It's like a book, I think, this bloomin' world,
Which you can read and care for just so long,
But presently you feel that you will die
Unless you get the page you're readin' done,
An' turn another—likely not so good;
But what you're after is to turn 'em all.

Gawd bless this world! Whatever she 'ath done—
Excep' when awful long—I've found it good.
So write, before I die, ' 'E liked it all!' "

and, having named that, I don't think I have missed much in "The Seven Seas."

4. *Scattered Poems.*

Since the publication of "The Seven Seas," Mr. Kipling has published in newspapers several poems, but the three which have made the deepest impression are: "The Vampire," the "Recessional," and "The White Man's Burden." "The Vampire" is something like a great achievement in satire, as it is surely the bitterest thing ever written by man against woman. The touch of hysteria in it, as of personal pain, will save women from taking it too much to heart; and, of course, like all recrimination between the sexes, it is necessarily one-sided. But all that discounts in no way from its murderous force.

With the "Recessional" and "The White Man's Burden" we enter upon a third period of Mr. Kipling's development as a poet—a period, to be sincere, with which, so far, poetry has little to do. It may be said that the "Recessional" and "The White Man's Burden" are more than poetry. I would venture to say that they are certainly less. In fact, they are not poetry at all, and it is uncritical, seriously, to consider them as such. They are political catch-words imbedded in rather spirited hymns, and they are in no sense the work of Rudyard Kipling the poet, but rather of Rudyard Kipling, unofficial M.P. for British Possessions. By writing them Mr. Kipling has become a greater political force than fifty members of Parliament, but not all the Great Powers, including Japan, can make them poetry. Their prestige is exactly that of "The Open Door," "Spheres of Influence," and such phrases; and the natural place for them was in a speech by Mr. Chamberlain, or—for a really graceful setting—Lord Rosebery. This is all I propose to say of them in this place.

5. *General.*

What, then, is the truth about Mr. Kipling's poetry, in this spring of 1899? It may, I think, be gathered from the running comment I have made in the previous pages. It is that Mr. Kipling is a master of captivating sing-song, a magician of catches and refrains. Of melodies that trip and dance, and gaily or mournfully or romantically come and go, there has, perhaps, been no such master before him in English; and he is this largely because he has had the wisdom to follow Burns, and write many of his ballads to popular or traditional airs, which must be allowed their share in the success. He is, so to say, the Burns, not of steam, but of the music-hall song.

"And the tunes that mean so much to you alone—
Common tunes that make you choke and blow your nose,
Vulgar tunes that bring the laugh that brings the groan—
I can rip your very heart-strings out with those."

Yes, in Mr. Kipling the banjo (self-admittedly his favourite instrument) has found its Apollo. Mr. Kipling can indeed wind our heart-strings round his little finger; but for joy or sorrow—or any manner of mystery—it must always be the banjo, and no other instrument. It must be either "*Pilly-willy-winky-winky popp*," or "*Tumpa-tumpa-tumpa-tum-pa tump*," or (for sorrow) "*Plunka-lunka-lunka-lunka-lunk*"; either that or—nothing. And, of course, seeing it is the banjo, there must always be dialect, not necessarily dialect of speech, but at least dialect of mood, dialect of the mind.

"The Vampire" is written in "essential" slang, and a devoted reading of everything Mr. Kipling has ever to my knowledge printed leads me to venture on the statement that, speaking of serious poetry, he has only written twelve non-dialect lines, and these are almost the best lines he has written. He buried them, as is his custom, in a *cache* —or he flew them kite-like with a long tail—of bad verses; but so poetry is often found:

"The depth and dream of my desire,
The bitter paths wherein I stray,

Thou knowest Who hast made the Fire,
  Thou knowest Who hast made the Clay.

One stone the more swings to her place
  In that dread Temple of Thy Worth—
It is enough that through Thy grace
  I saw naught common on Thy earth.

Take not that vision from my ken;
  Oh whatsoe'er may spoil or speed,
Help me to need no aid from men
  That I may help such men as need."

But these notwithstanding, I venture, without great consciousness of daring, to state that in the high calm zones of poetry, where a word lasts for a thousand years; where a thought needs no renewal of temporary slang to give it piquant edge; where the mystery of things is deep and simple as at the beginning; where the poet's voice is so strong and clear that it needs no modern devices to make it carry; where the languages of Babylon and Persia and Egypt and Rome and Greece and Italy and England are but as dialects of one eternal speech; in zones where you put the earth in one line, the sea in another, and sun, moon, and stars in a third; in the zones where Homer sings immortally of war, though it was never given to his poor blind eyes to dote on a gun-cotton gun or a submarine boat; where Shakespeare knows all about the world, though three-fourths of it is yet to be discovered; where Keats knows all beauty, though he is quite ignorant of Greek: into these zones, I am sure, Mr. Kipling—with that absence of arrogance which characterises one who is decidedly the most famous of our younger men of letters—will be only too glad to be admitted as an Academy student.

CHAPTER II

THE STORIES

1. "Plain Tales from the Hills."

2. "Soldiers Three," "The Story of the Gadsbys," "In Black and White."

3. "Wee Willie Winkie," "Under the Deodars," "The Phantom 'Rickshaw and Other Stories."

4. "The Light that Failed."

5. "Life's Handicap, being Stories of Mine Own People."

6. "Many Inventions."

7. "The Jungle Book."

8. "The Second Jungle Book."

9. "Captains Courageous: a Story of the Grand Banks."

10. "The Day's Work."

Six volumes of short stories, including stories told in dialogue; one novel; two fairy-tale books, and one boy's book. Such is the material for our consideration of Mr. Kipling as a story-teller, counting by the English editions, and disregarding "The Naulahka" and "Stalky & Co.," perhaps the best school story ever written, and concerning which it is sufficient against objectors to quote Mr. Kipling's own criticism: "It's not brutality . . . It's boy; only boy."

I

The short stories number one hundred and thirty-one. Of these no less than forty are included in "Plain Tales," which, having been contributed originally (at least twenty-eight of them) to *The Civil and Military Gazette*, are all, no doubt for that reason, much shorter than Mr. Kipling's other stories. Evidently, journalistic conditions kept them down to an average of some two thousand words apiece; and that insistence on a comprehensive brevity is always something to the credit of journalism as a literary training. " In every poem, train the leading shoot, break off the suckers," runs a dictum of Landor's. There is nothing like journalism for breaking off the suckers, and as Mr. Kipling's style is essentially a journalistic one, journalism at its highest power, the journalism of a man of genius, journalism vitalised by an imagination which usually reserves itself for higher forms of prose, this reference to *The Civil and Military Gazette*—as an earlier reference to Mr. Kipling's newspaper office experiences—is not without its significance.

Of these one hundred and thirty-one stories, one hundred and twelve, from one point of view or another, are stories of life in India. Of the remaining nineteen, five are sea-stories; four, yarns of life trading and botanising in South America; two are allegories (" The Finest Story in the World" and " Children of the Zodiac"); two are what may be called " fairy-tales of science";

one is a story of a South American republic; two are stories of Americans in England; one is a story of Americans in America; one is a Whitechapel story, and one I can only describe as "Brugglesmith."

Two main determinations run through these stories, as through the whole of Mr. Kipling's work: to celebrate the romance of the English Government of India; and to celebrate the romance of commerce throughout the world—generally speaking, the heroism of modern life. In this, of course, Mr. Kipling is not a pioneer; but, perhaps, his work provides the most concrete embodiment yet given us of an ideal common to many poets and essayists and novelists of the last twenty years, and voiced most aggressively by Walt Whitman. But while the others say: "Modern life is as heroic as any," Mr. Kipling is most ready with convincing examples. Young as he still is, and vigourous as he is likely to remain for many coming years, it is not unlikely that, section by section, he may make a complete picture of British and American rule, and thus become the snap-shot Balzac of Anglo-Saxon colonisation—his gifts for getting up a country and its people are so exceptional. Yet it seems unlikely, judging by his essays in new fields, that he will ever do, say, America or Australia as he has done India. Evident as is his note-book sometimes in his Indian sketches, it is less that than his sub-conscious experience and memory of the country that counts. There are, too, his father's affectionately acknowledged stores of Indian lore and anecdote to be remembered. One cannot be a boy in two countries at once, and there is little doubt that Mr. Kipling's best work will always be Indian in subject, however heroically he may strive to span the octave of the globe.

The consideration of his prose work then practically resolves itself into a consideration of his aim to write the romance of the

English government of India. Necessarily three persons are chiefly concerned in that romance: the English official, the English soldier, and the native. Already in "Departmental Ditties" we have seen Mr. Kipling's youthful satire at work upon home ignorance of the Anglo-Indian official lot. Not the ignorance merely, but the indifference of the comfortable Englishman to all that distant dog's work and danger, seems early and late to have impressed Mr. Kipling with its injustice and stupidity. Here was an empire purchased at what cost, maintained at what expenditure of brain and blood and treasure, momentous, maybe, to the very existence of the British Empire—and yet to the peace-lulled people of England a matter of incredible indifference. Old the tale of how it was won, old already, too, the tale of how it was nearly lost, old Thackeray's begums and colonels. Its conquest had been exciting, but its maintenance was the business—the prosaic business—of the Indian Civil Service. Even the Supreme Government itself slept upon Indian affairs, only awakening at times to impede by its ignorance the work of those who know—comparatively—in Calcutta.

"Gentlemen come from England," writes Mr. Kipling in a passage which might serve as a text for a large section of his work, "spend a few weeks in India, walk round this great Sphinx of the Plains, and write books upon its ways and its works, denouncing or praising it as their own ignorance prompts. Consequently all the world knows how the Supreme Government conducts itself. But no one, not even the Supreme Government, knows everything about the administration of the Empire. Year by year England sends out fresh drafts for the first fighting-line, which is officially called the Indian Civil Service. These die, or kill themselves by overwork, or are worried to death or broken in health and hope in order that the land may be protected from death and sickness, famine and war, and may eventually become capable of standing alone. It will never stand alone; but the idea is a pretty one, and men are willing to die for it, and yearly the work of pushing and coaxing and scolding and petting the country into good living goes forward. If an advance be made all credit is given to the native, while the Englishmen stand back and wipe their foreheads. If a failure occurs the Englishmen step forward and take the blame."

It is from the lives of such Englishmen—their pluck and patience, their hard-earned adulteries at Simla, and their occasional excursions "across the pale" into the mystery-land of native India—that Mr. Kipling has gathered so many of his vivid anecdotes. A great number of them (certainly most of the "Plain Tales"), considered singly, are "departmental" in the narrow sense. Their appeal is chiefly to those who have gone through the same mill. Taken separately they are, so to speak, somebody else's shop, interesting to read once, as brightly told shop always is; but with nothing in their treatment to make us wish to read them again. If Mr. Kipling did not sometimes discover India universally human, as well as gossipingly "departmental," their value would be already exhausted.

Considered, however, not singly, but as contributing, however slightly, to that episodical epic of India which it has been Mr. Kipling's ambition to write, they have their place. They are the lesser lights and darks contributing to such more serious elements of the general picture as "At the End of the Passage," "Without Benefit of Clergy," "In Flood Time," "The Man Who Was," behind which looms vast in the background the image of that old Sphinx of the Plains complete in mystery as no other writer has ever been able to suggest her.

A sphinx, too, of so many meanings.

In emphasising that Mr. Kipling has done a great service to Viceroys. To us at home India is long ago a conquest; to the Anglo-Indian, on the contrary, it has daily to be conquered. We say "India," as though India were a unity, instead of a congeries of mutually hostile kingdoms, divided broadly, to start with, on the bitter religious feud between Mohammedan and Hindu, and, after that, infinitesimally complicated in a venomous tangle of race-hatreds and fierce ancestral distinctions. To keep the teeth of India from the throat of India is one of the initial difficulties of Indian administration. Not realising this, many well-meaning Viceroys make beautiful mistakes, as, for instance, when, in the story of "The Head of the District," the "Very Greatest of All the Viceroys" appointed a distinguished Bengali to the government of a turbulent hill-district. Mr. Grish Chunder Dé, M.A., was as English as an English university could make him; his talk was of bump-suppers, cricket matches, and hunting-runs. He would say "We must get these fellows in hand," and in every respect he was terribly English. But that sort of thing could not deceive the Khusru Kheyl. Mr. Grish Chunder Dé, M.A., remained a Bengali, and being that, dirt beneath the feet of all Hindustan. "Has the government gone mad to send a black Bengali dog to us?" asked the righteously indignant chief of the clan. Such is the fate of sentimental government in India. "A child of the country to the rule of the country." What could be prettier —in theory? But then "what looks so feasible in Calcutta, so right in Bombay, so unassailable in Madras, is misunderstood by the North, and entirely changes its complexion on the banks of the Indus."

Few writers so well illustrate the old artistic maxim that the part is greater than the whole than Mr. Kipling in writing of India. Rich as he is in minutiæ, it is, after all, as invariably in potent description, the phrase that tells. "The stern, black-bearded kings who sit about the Council-board of India"; "Look, there are the lights of the mail-train going to Peshawur!" It is in such flash-light phrases that Mr. Kipling reveals India to our imaginations. One might say that in those two sentences are contained the extremes of modern India. To say them over to one's self is to see again many other pictures of Mr. Kipling's Indian panorama. Between those phrases lie the India of "the blazing sky, the dried-up over-handled earth," the India of "At the End of the Passage":

"The men flung themselves down, ordering the punkah-coolies by all the powers of Hell to pull. Every door and window was shut, for the outside air was that of an oven. The atmosphere within was only 104°, as the thermometer bore witness, and heavy with the foul smell of badly-trimmed kerosene lamps; and this stench, combined with that of native tobacco, baked brick, and dried earth, sends the heart of many a strong man down to his boots, for it is the smell of the Great Indian Empire when she turns herself for six months into a house of torment"; the famine-stricken India of "William the Conqueror," the moon-haunted India of "The Strange Ride of Morrowbie Jukes."

Then what glimpses we get of the absurdities of Indian government in a flash of satire such as this: "Even the Secretariat believes that it does good when it asks an over-driven Executive Officer to take a census of wheat-weevils through a district of five thousand square miles"; and particularly in that delightful bit of farce called "Pig."

Above all things, perhaps, Mr. Kipling makes us realise the cruel heat of India. Surely "The City of Dreadful Night" is, literally, the hottest story ever written.

There is not a breath of air stirring from beginning to end.

One would think it a country too hot for Englishmen to love in. But, indeed, no. As befits a true impression, the all-pervading presence of woman is here too; and story after story illustrates woman as the goddess in the great machine of Anglo-Indian government. These men sweat and count up their weevils—for some woman. If they rise high in the service, be sure Mrs. Hauksbee is somewhere behind; if they go under, suspect Mrs. Reiver; and, in addition to civilised, flirtatious woman, there is always the so-called "brown" woman, "fair as bar gold," on whom Mr. Kipling seems to have lavished nearly all the tenderness he has to spare for women as a sex, and "niggers" as a race—which really means that he knows and loves essential woman, who is always best as a simple, gentle savage, with no pretence to masculine "civilisation."

"I've a neater, sweeter maiden in a cleaner, greener land"—

apparently represents Mr. Kipling's own leanings on the most important of all subjects. Generally speaking, though one mustn't forget the delightful exception of "William the Conqueror," his civilised woman is represented by "The Vampire," the vampire for whom poor Wressley of the Foreign Office wrote his great book, an absurd tribute of the intellect at the feet of the sensual doll.

In the "romance of the clash of civilisations" (to quote a phrase of Mr. Grant Allen's, whose "Rev. John Creedy" was a notable pioneer of the *genre*) Mr. Kipling's India is rich; that India of picturesque and terrible superstitions, busy and muttering in the darkness on either side of the Peshawur express, the India of black magic, as "In the House of Suddhoo":

"A stone's throw out on either hand
From that well-ordered road we tread,
And all the world is wild and strange:
Churel and ghoul and *Djinn* and sprite
Shall bear us company to-night,
For we have reached the Oldest Land
Wherein the Powers of Darkness range—"

the India of monkey gods and elephant gods, whom it is still far from safe to insult, as we may read in "The Mark of the Beast": the India, on one side, of Strickland (the Waring-like experimentalist in Indian life) and, on the other, of Mowgli.

Of the native himself Mr. Kipling's view is mainly the view of his hero Tommy Atkins. God made Hindus for the British soldier to wipe his feet on, and Afridis for the British soldier to bayonet "with deep hacking coughs." Certain noble child-like traits are recorded of them sparingly, and we have a glimpse of one District Commissioner who, in the phrase of the land, felt really like "a father and a mother" to the wild hill-people under his care. Then, too, we must not forget the gentle vision (out of "William the Conqueror") of Scott sneezing in the dust of a hundred little feet, his "Kindergarten" of tiny famine-stricken Hindus, and his walking amongst them at sunset, "a god in a halo of golden dust, walking slowly at the head of his flocks, while at his knee ran small naked Cupids."

Like a true Englishman, Mr. Kipling loves to pretend that he has no feelings, and, like a true Englishman, there are occasions when his feelings are certainly inadequate; but, all the same, we must be a little careful sometimes in taking his cynicism and hard-heartedness at their surface values. Sometimes, at least, they are dramatic. Yet, with his sympathies so evidently akin to those of his hero, he cannot blame us if sometimes we identify his dramatic utterances with his personal feelings.

As for his pictures of that "very strong man," it is for intelligent officers to speak of their accuracy. A mere civilian is, necessarily, no judge of that. One evidence in favour of their truth is that, with all Mr. Kipling's good-will, they are usually far from flattering:

> ". . . single men in barricks don't grow
> into plaster saints."

The particular Tommies Mr. Kipling singles out are certainly "no thin, red 'eroes." When a man does an heroic action he is usually able to give a good unheroic reason for it, as in the story called "In the Matter of a Private"; and as for the Three Musketeers *de nos jours*, Mulvaney may be true to one individual life, but it has been the custom in all countries and times to promote such exceptionally charming beings from the rank and file of mortality to the bright legions of mythology. There are men of genius and charm and good heart in all callings, but they are always *sui generis*, and in no way typical of the callings to which they accidentally belong. Mulvaney, indeed, illustrates that idealising, somewhat sentimental, side of Mr. Kipling's art, which alternates, rather surprisingly, with the realistic, cynical side. Should some commentator answer this remark with Mulvaney's real name and address, Mulvaney would no less remain a figure of romance. Besides, Mr. Kipling's typical British soldier is Irish!

Probably Ortheris, so far as we can individualise him, is more typical of the British Tommy, and he is nothing like so attractive. Learoyd is little more than a battering-ram with a Yorkshire dialect. Yet there is one remark of his, with Mulvaney's and Ortheris's comments upon it, which may serve as a text for Mr. Kipling's vindication of the British soldier, disregarded no less by a peace-loving, war-waging people, than is the obscure Anglo-Indian official whom he supports with his rifle:

"They talk o' rich folk bein' stuck up an' genteel," says Learoyd, telling the story of his heart, "but for cast-iron pride o' respectability there's naught like poor chapel folk. It's as cold as th' wind o' Greenhow Hill—ay, and colder, for 'twill never change. And now I come to think on it, one at strangest things I know is 'at they couldn't abide th' thought o' soldiering. There's a vast o' fightin' i' th' Bible, and there's a deal of Methodists i' th' Army; but to hear chapel folk talk yo'd think that soldierin' were next door, an' t'other side, to hangin'. . . . And they'd tell tales in th' Sunday-school o' bad lads as had been thumped and brayed for bird-nesting o' Sundays and playin' truant o' week-days, and how they took to wrestlin', dog fightin', rabbit-runnin', and drinkin', till at last, as if 'twere a hepitaph on a gravestone, they damned him across th' moors wi', 'an then he went and 'listed for a soldier,' an' they'd all fetch a deep breath, and throw up their eyes like a hen drinkin'.'

"'Fwhy is ut?' said Mulvaney, bringing down his hand on his thigh with a crack. 'In the name av God, fwhy is ut? I've seen ut, tu. They cheat an' they swindle, an' they lie an' they slander, an' fifty things fifty times worse; but the last an' the worst by their reckonin' is to serve the Widdy honest. It's like the talk av childer—seein' things all round.'

"'Plucky lot of fightin' good fights of whatsername they'd do if we didn't see they had a quiet place to fight in. And such fightin' as theirs is! Cats on the tiles. T'other callin' to which to come on . . .' said Ortheris with an oath."

Yet, though India is the subject-matter which best suits Mr. Kipling's hand, as another man will write best of Greece, another of "Wessex," and another of "Thrums," and though that choice of subject-matter was a fortunate accident of birth so far as Mr. Kipling's contemporary vogue is concerned, it was, perhaps, rather in spite of, than because of his subject, that he was most enthusiastically read by those whose enthusiasm matters most in the end. So far as literature is concerned, India owes more to Mr. Kipling than he to India. In whatever environment he had hatched out, his voracity for knowledge would no less have eaten up his surroundings—to spin in the end no less brilliant a literary cocoon.

Seriously speaking, it is rather a pity for literature that he was thus born in a sensational province of the empire, as it was a pity for so great a natural gift as that of Burns to be born into the Scotch dialect, or as it is a pity that so many gifts of similarly vivid impressionism should be born into American journalism. Important to us as India is to-day, and as it will continue to remain for a few to-morrows, its importance is only a passing crisis in those strategical and commercial complications of the human race which change nothing in that human nature with which lasting writings are concerned. India has its lasting importance in literature—the importance of its sacred books. Mr. Kipling's stories, as subject-matter, are merely the cables of a brilliant journalist describing the long-drawn looting of an ancient civilisation. The circumstances are of no original importance. "When India belongs to Russia," said a distinguished poet to the present writer, "no one will understand Kipling." At all events, he will certainly need a glossary. Yes, only in so far as the stories are universally human, as well as Indian, will they—and do they—really matter. How far they are that we may, perhaps, measure by considering them not as Indian stories, but just as *stories*. I do not propose to examine them exhaustively or on any set principles, but by recording several impressions of the stories as a whole I may, perhaps, best suggest a tentative conclusion. Yet if occasionally I should seem to hint at, or even be compelled to refer to, general principles, such references may, I hope, seem inevitable to some few readers.

Perhaps the quality that first struck one in reading Mr. Kipling's stories was their exceptional reality—*while you read them.* That, and the extraordinary knowledge not only of the details of human life, but of its less speedily learnt moods, complications, and significances; knowledge, too, that, even in a generation so inured to marvellous boys, was made the more astonishing by its precocious acquirement. There was, indeed, a conscious and irritating air of knowingness; as, for example, here: "Michele was working in his office when he heard the sound that a man never forgets all his life, the '*ah-yah*' of an angry crowd. [When that sound drops about three tones, and changes to a thick, droning *ut*, the man who hears it had better go away if he is alone.]" This is, indeed, calculated to impress, and yet, in spite of these boyish airs of omniscience, it was evident that Mr. Kipling had read deeply in the book of human life. He really did know an astonishing number of things about men and women, white and brown.

It was almost uncanny to hear this Chatterton of India talking after this fashion: "Now, a Dalesman from beyond Skipton will forgive an injury when the Strid lets a man live; but a South Devon man is as soft as a Dartmoor bog"; "I have seen Captain Hayes argue with a tough horse—I have seen a tonga-driver coerce a stubborn pony—I have seen a riotous setter broken to gun by a hard keeper . . ."; "Did you ever know Shackles—b. w. g., 15. 1⅜—coarse, loose, mule-like ears—barrel as long as a gate-post—tough as a telegraph-wire—and the queerest brute that ever looked through a bridle? He was of no brand, being one of an ear-nicked mob taken into the *Bucephalus* at £4 10*s*. a head to make up freight, and sold raw and out of condition at Calcutta for Rs. 275."; "The women sang the Song of the Pick—the terrible, slow, swinging melody with the muttered chorus that repeats the sliding of the loosened coal, and, to each cadence, Kundoo smote in the black dark"; "Listen! I see it all—down, down even to the stays! *Such* stays! Six-eight a pair, Polly, with red flannel—or list, is it?—that they put into the tops of those fearful things." The way of "Queenstown potato-smacks in a runnin' tide," the danger of poking a camp-fire with a bayonet, the window decorations of Aylesbury dairies, the secret talk of women as they unhook their stays with a sigh of relief after a ball, the meaning (hidden from his readers) of "T. Gs," and "E. P. tents," the hardness of "five-year-old tea-baulks," and, apparently, all the heart of man and the whole heartlessness of woman: was there anything this youngster had not seen, done, or remembered?

Then he was evidently a born story-teller. To him had been given the wonderful knack of doing with the pen what so many delightful men, quite inglorious and often hardly respectable, do daily in bar-parlours and other haunts of anecdote, by fleeting fascinating word of mouth. Indeed, here was just that very method captured in literature—the vividness, the nearness, the endearing, or irritating, slang of it. The last minstrel of the bar-parlour; the fish-liar of the smoking-room; the flash-light man of American journalism; the English "public-school" man, who brilliantly "don't you knows" his way through a story: here were all these, plus that "something, something" of genius that makes "not a fourth sound, but a star."

A humourist, too, at once simple and subtle. Perhaps farce is the test of your true humourist; and, over and over again, Mr. Kipling was convicted of a delightful boyish love of farce. Serious realists have reproached him, I see, for such revelries of fun as "The Incarnation of Krishna Mulvaney." As if anything in the world couldn't happen to Mulvaney—Mulvaney drunk, with his heels kicking out of a queen's palanquin to begin the story.

Also he had written at least one love-story ("Without Benefit of Clergy") that broke one's heart; and ghost-stories, and tales of so-called "supernatural" horror, which, in spite of traditional expedients (such as "It" and "The Thing," and dogs barking at the unseen, and horses plunging, and the breaking of the photographic plates in "At the End of the Passage"—as obvious a begging of the mystery as that which Stevenson has pointed out in the "impressively" reticent conclusion of "The Pit and the Pendulum"), really got hold of one. One may pause to remark that this vein of "supernaturalism" is very characteristic of Mr. Kipling; and that related to it the theory of previous incarnations seems to have considerable attraction for him. Witness "The Brushwood Boy," one of his best love-stories. One may note, too, his interest in insanity and morbid states of mind.

In "The Gadsbys" was some of the most brilliantly exact social dialogue written in recent years.

Then there were touching child-stories, which you fancied or not; there were the two "Jungle Books," not unlikely the most enduring things Mr. Kipling has written: and, if the stories had left us with no other gain, they had given us one lifelong companion, Terence Mulvaney.

Scattered here and there among the stories were remarkable descriptions, pictures, and picturesque phrases, much wit, and many kinds of wisdom. Such was our first, and, in many respects, lasting impression.

II

In speaking of the remarkable sense of reality conveyed by Mr. Kipling's stories, I added, "while you read them"; and, gratefully recording the one impression, I must be allowed also to record that which, unexpectedly enough, is its complement. The stories are full of surprises, but one great and disappointing surprise is the facility with which we forget them. Paper and print have seldom, if ever, produced so magic-lantern-like an impression of reality. One is the more surprised to find how skilfully they elude the memory. Out of all these one hundred and thirty-one stories, there is not more than a dozen of which a normal memory can recall the features, and, numerous as are the characters to which we have been introduced, there are certainly not half-a-dozen whom we can differentiate. I think that one reason for this in the case of many of the stories, is to be found in the slightness of narrative motive. They are glorified anecdotes, for the most part, and, as in the case of those oral *raconteurs* to whom I have referred, they exist only in the skilful telling. But there is still another, and, perhaps, more important, reason.

Is it not a question of methods, and are not the stories that most live with us just those that are less markedly "Kiplingesque," and more related to traditional methods of story-telling? Broadly speaking, it is the Mulvaney stories that we remember best; those, and two or three pictures written in comparatively classical English, such as "The Gate of the Hundred Sorrows" and "The City of Dreadful Night."

Now, limited as a medium as is the Irish dialect, it is classical compared with the idiom in which most of Mr. Kipling's stories are told. There are English dialects for which so far even conspicuous literary talent has failed to win permanent acceptance in serious literature. William Barnes would have been recognised as a poet of considerable importance had he not chosen to write in Dorsetshire; and Edwin Waugh was a humourist of genius and a poet of real charm, who has taken the consequences of hiding his light under the bushel of the Lancashire dialect. Nor is the Welsh way of breaking English acceptable in literature. What we call "Irish" and "Scotch," however, have managed to win recognition for themselves as literary media; it remains to be seen whether Mr. Kipling will be able to win like permanent recognition for "Cockney." It will surely be posterity's loss rather than his if it should prove otherwise.

An Irishman's way of telling a story is among the accepted traditional forms of story-telling, like the manner of the Arabian Nights. Also, however original an Irish character may be, he is already more than half made with his dialect. Thus Mulvaney may be the most delightful Irishman who ever lived in a book, but, whether that is so or not, his road to our hearts has already been more than half made by many a delightful forerunner in Lever or Lover. He is a development, a variation of a traditional type, rather than a creation. And, perhaps, one may as well say here, once for all, that Mr. Kipling possesses but little power of creating character. He is deft at giving you sufficient notion of this man or that woman to last out their story. But mainly the story is the thing, and the characters are little more than pegs on which to hang an anecdote.

One's memory of a novelist's names and one's memory of his characters go together. One never forgets the name of a really memorable figure in a book. All the lasting story-tellers will bear this test. Of living men take George Meredith, Thomas Hardy, and J. M. Barrie; and, out of England, Tolstoi, Zola, and Ibsen. Or take the novelist with whose name Mr. Kipling's is so often mentioned, Dickens. Perhaps no other novelist has ever created so many living names. The names, some may say, are more real than the people. But that depends on one's test of reality. If one's test is the test of the occurrence of Dickensonian characters in what we call real life, it is narrow and irrelevant; for some of the most living creations of literature have never existed, nor ever will exist anywhere but in the imagination of novelist and reader. Is anyone going to deny the reality of Mr. Micawber on any such shallow grounds? His name comes so readily to one's lips because he is so imaginative a reality. Have we a friend of whose identity we are so absolutely sure? Maybe he has never yet been met in the Strand, nor shall we meet him; but were we to do so, should we have a moment's doubt as to his identity? "Why, it's Mr. Micawber!" we would exclaim excitedly, as though it were the ghost of Mr. Gladstone.

We might recognise Mulvaney in the same way, but of all Mr. Kipling's *dramatis personæ*, he is the one alone, and very genuinely isolated, of whom we would thus be sure: and then it would not be so much because he was Mulvaney, as because he was an unmistakable Irishman. And yet, if that be true, is there any other Irishman in fiction we would more gladly meet? How fascinating he is, with all his contrasts of nature; his blackguardism, his chivalry, his gallantry, his folly, his wisdom, his never-failing humour, and his ever-lurking melancholy. It is of such contrasts that the true human clay is kneaded. Someone should make a "Book of the Wisdom of Terence Mulvaney." It would take a high place in *pensée* literature. I append a small collection towards it.

This self-picture might be included by way of introducing the sage: "I'm a born scutt av the barrick-room! The Army's mate an' dhrink to me, bekaze I'm wan av the few that can't quit ut. I've put in siv-inteen years, an' the pipeclay's in the mar-row av me. Av I cud have kept out av wan big dhrink a month, I wud have been a Hon'ry Lift'nint by this time—a nuisince to my betthers, a laughin'-shtock to my equils, an' a curse to meself. Bein' fwhat I am, I'm Privit Mulvaney, wid no good-conduc' pay an' a devourin' thirst. Always barrin' me little frind Bobs Bahadur, I know as much about the Army as most men."

Here beginneth the Wisdom, etc.: "Hit a man an' help a woman, an' ye can't be far wrong anyways;"—"But I've had my day—I've had my day, an' nothin' can take away the taste av that! O my time past, whin I put me fut through ivry livin' wan av the Tin Commandmints between Revelly and Lights Out, blew the froth off a pew-ter, wiped me moustache wid the back av me hand, an' slept on ut all as quiet as a little child! But ut's over—ut's over, an' 'twill niver come back to me; not though I prayed for a week av Sundays;"—"Kape out av the Married Quarters, I say, as I did not. 'Tis onwholesim, 'tis dangerous, an' 'tis ivrything else that's bad, but—O my sowl, 'tis swate while ut lasts!"—"Watch the hand: av she shuts her hand tight, thumb down over the knuckle, take up your hat an' go. You'll only make a fool av yoursilf av you shtay. But av the hand lies opin on the lap, or av you see her thryin' to shut ut, an' she can't,—go on. She's not past reason' wid;"—"Afther they was all gone, I wint back to Canteen an' called for a quart to put a thought in me;"—"I am av the opinion av Polonius whin he said, Don't fight wid ivry scutt for the pure joy av fightin', but if you do, knock the nose av him first an' frequint;"—"Good cause the reg'ment has to know me for the best soldier in ut. Better cause have I to know mesilf for the worst man. I'm only fit to tache the new drafts what I'll niver learn myself;"—"Niver show a woman that ye care the snap av a finger for her, an' begad she'll come bleatin' to your boot-heels!"—"I kissed her on the tip av the nose an' undher the eye; an' a girl that lets a kiss come tumbleways like that has never been kissed before. Take note av that, sorr;"—"They'll take the airs an' the graces instid av the man nine times out av ten, an' they only find the blunder later—the wimmen;"—"Whin liquor does not take hould, the sowl av a man is rotten in him."

Mulvaney's is that effortless life which belongs to all really vital creations of fiction. It would seem that the more pains Mr. Kipling takes with his characters the less they live. For example, take the fishermen in "Captains Courageous." How hard Mr. Kipling strove to distinguish and vitalise them is written all over them, and yet, with the partial exception of the captain, the most careful reading has failed to fix them in the memory.

"Soldiers Three" then (and I include under that head all the Mulvaney stories), in my opinion, represents Mr. Kipling's most important achievement in prose; and it will be observed that once more, as in his verse, the achievement is in dialect. Yet it is a dialect which, it is important to insist, is more "classical" as a medium than the journalistic, mess-room, public-school English in which the majority of Mr. Kipling's stories are written. In the Mulvaney stories the reality is that of a more universal humanity. The humour and wit and pathos are concerned with the general heart of man. Lasting art (and Mr. Kipling must forgive the term) is concerned rather with generals than particulars, or only such particulars, so to speak, as are general. True imaginative literature is symbolic rather than scientific. The best of Mr. Kipling's stories are symbolic; the majority are scientific. Contrast, say, "The Courting of Dinah Shadd" and "The Bridge-Builders," both good things in their way. One is a *genre* painting rich in the humour and romance of a broad, enduring humanity; the other is a brilliant cinematographic reproduction of a specialised ambition in action.

In the latter case (leaving out of account the clumsy and long-drawn mythologising at the end) we see *a* bridge and *a* bridge-builder with daylight clearness. It is what the man in the street would call as "true to life" as writing can be. But can anyone, not morbidly memorial, tell me the name of the bridge-builder, or, with or without a name, will he think of him as *the* bridge-builder, as one thinks of *the* "Master-Builder" out of Ibsen, or such a type of that modern commercial romance Mr. Kipling essays to write as John Gabriel Borkman?

Yes, most of Mr. Kipling's stories (and

probably those which have most advanced his general reputation) belong to science rather than to art. If I say that they are the product of the literary faculty anticipating the cinematograph, it is by no means with the intention of minimising their wonderfulness, but rather that I may the more clearly indicate the kind of wonderfulness that really belongs to them. They belong to the wonders of science rather than the wonders of art—that science of instinctive human faculty which anticipates all inventions; that marvellous science of literal mimicry and piquantly faithful record which finds its most attractive expression, perhaps, on the music-hall stage. It is only those who have not realised the wonderfulness of Yvette Guilbert or of Mr. Arthur Roberts who will think my comparison of Mr. Kipling to those artists frivolous or disrespectful. I am sure that Mr. Kipling himself will make no such mistake. So, curiously enough, and without premeditation, I find that Mr. Kipling's prose as well as his verse sends me to the music-halls for final illustration.

I have not meant in these remarks merely to repeat a familiar criticism of Mr. Kipling that his work is "photographic," for, while in one sense the criticism is true, in another it is unjust. And the distinction is an interesting one. In his effects Mr. Kipling is usually photographic ("cinematographic" is better), but his methods are almost invariably, for want of a better word, "artistic." I mean that whereas the principle of selection, which is a vital principle of art, can operate but little in photography, it is seen to be remarkably active in all Mr. Kipling's best work. His stories, so to speak, represent the epigram of action, the epigram of a given situation. One thinks of a Phil May—a Phil May, however, whose line is not merely marvellously selected from a hundred other irrelevant lines, but is also subtly charged with an experience, a poetry, and a general suggestiveness, which Mr. Phil May's line does not possess.

I am thrown upon analogies to other arts and sciences in writing of Mr. Kipling, because literary analogies are difficult. Speaking merely of his literary method, he belongs to the same modern, rebellious school as Carlyle or Browning, a school determined to say the eternal thing in the contemporary way, and yet say it eternally too. On the other side are the more traditional methods of Tennyson and Arnold. How far Carlyle or Browning will be able to force understanding of their brusque and piquant nineteenth-century slang, upon a posterity thrilling to the brusquerie and piquancy of its own momentary manner of speech, is a question impossible to answer; but it is obvious that, if the primal force in Carlyle or Browning is greater than in Tennyson or Arnold, they will surely need it all.

But to return to my first analogy. It is among the anomalies and ironies of art that Mr. Kipling thus uses so brilliantly, often so masterly, the methods of art for the production of work which, in the end, affects us mainly as photography. Place a story of his and a story, say, of Stevenson's before an audience, as one might place a cinematograph impression and an old master, and who can doubt whose story would win applause for the sense of immediate reality, of literality of impression?

Or to take another writer from whom Mr. Kipling has learned much, and with whom, perhaps, he is more appropriately compared, Mr. Bret Harte. Bear in mind, I am not talking of posterity, but of contemporary judgments and memories. At the moment Mr. Kipling may seem so much more vivid and "true to life"; and yet, while it is, at most, ten years since we began to read him, and more than ten since we left off reading Bret Harte, it is not deniable that we remember the first story we read by Bret Harte better than the last read story of Rudyard Kipling. Both men are artists in their methods, but one gave us pictures, and the other, mainly, cinematography. Mr. Kipling is a great man at sentiment (though we hear more of his anti-sentimental side), but has he written a child-story we can remember as well as "The Luck of Roaring Camp," or anything we shall remember as long as "The Outcasts of Poker Flat," or "Tennessee's Pardner"? These things are not so exact in their "business" (to borrow a term from still another art), but, perhaps on that very account, they remain symbols of the human heart. They have the simplicity of classics, a simplicity in which all unnecessary subtleties are dissolved; and simplicity is the quality which, out of all the seething elements of creation, the brilliant observation, the subtle charging with modern moods, the various miracles of process, Mr. Kipling is too clever to capture except in one or two supreme moments.

Seeing that the essence of Mr. Kipling's method is his unerring choice of the telling characteristic, and, so to say, the poster word, his robust rejection of all but the essential, it is surprising to notice in his more recent work, side by side with the same keen eye and sure hand, a curious, but perhaps not incomprehensible, tendency to debauch on the part of one of his most notable gifts. His "mastery of detail," as we say, has been one of his marvels from the beginning; but, though in some of his ballads, as I have remarked, his gift sometimes escaped control in a riot of technicalities, for the most part in his early best stories (and nearly all his best work was done at the beginning), it was a magical servant. Of late, however, it is unmistakably becoming a dreary master. In writing of India, or soldiers, Mr. Kipling was often necessarily "departmental," but he was seldom, if ever, microscopically technical, as he has suddenly become in attempting to fulfil that second half or nis programme, "to celebrate the romance of commerce throughout the world."

In spite of Learoyd's occasional suspicious allusions to the note-book, there is little untransmuted note-book in the Indian stories. There is more of it in the "Barrack-Room Ballads." On the other hand, in his stories of the sea, or, say, merchant shipping, undigested note-book is everywhere in evidence. For Mr. Kipling to write a story without some firm human touch, however slight, would be impossible. I have read all he has printed either with pleasure, or pleasurable irritation, and I am not ungrateful for the crumbs which fall from the master's table even at his most meagre banquets. But if Mr. Kipling is never quite dull or unprofitable, he comes perilously near to it in such stories as "Captains Courageous," "Bread Upon the Waters," "The Ship that Found Herself," and "·007."

"Captains Courageous" is Mr. Kipling's second attempt (or, if we count the collaborated "Naulahka") the third to oblige those critics who always egg a writer on to do just that for which he has little gift and less inclination. I suppose it was because Mr. Kipling's narrative genius was so evidently created for the short story, that those critics immediately cried out for a novel. One might hazard that Mr. Kipling has never really wished to write a novel, perhaps has never confidently believed that he could, or clearly seen why he should. But the barren critic, with his cuckoo cry, insisted; said that the public expected it; and Mr. Kipling obliged with "The Light that Failed"—a novel which, in spite of Mr. Kipling's evident uneasiness at having to use so many words where he could have told the whole thing in at least five thousand, is more of an achievement than has yet been sufficiently recognised. In "Maisie" and the red-haired girl it gives us the two most living women Mr. Kipling has drawn—the first another bitter—tender study for "The Vampire"; and the description of Dick Heldar's blindness was a masterpiece of the dramatic imagination. Milton has put his blindness into a few famous lines, and there are pages of "Jane Eyre." Nowhere else that I know of has the hopelessness of blindness been so brought home to us; and, one may pertinently add, a modern blindness. For Dick Heldar was one of those for whom, as Gautier said, the visible world exists—and that only; he had not Milton's advantage of believing in an invisible world as well—an advantage impossible to exaggerate for the blind. "The Light that Failed" is, perhaps, the story of all Mr. Kipling's stories that strikes the most universal note of human pathos.

"Captains Courageous," Mr. Kipling's

first really determined attempt to write the prose epic of merchant shipping, is "another story." Here, to begin with, Mr. Kipling is, for once, dramatically unequal to his central motive—a failure seldom known of him. Given an objectionable American youngster millionnaire crossing to England on a liner, entirely foolish with wealth and the electro-plated snobbery of his country —sweep him overboard one rough day on to the deck of one of those Newfoundland cod-fishers, which (with those tendencies to spectacular butchery which wealth seems to have engendered in all civilisations) he had been hoping they might run down for an excitement; confront him with a stern old Ironsides of a skipper, who cares nothing about his fine airs, and isn't worldly enough to see the money behind his swagger: well, if not thrilling, it was an allowably interesting situation. The testing of the lad's mettle might have made an interesting study in human training. Unfortunately, however, Mr. Kipling begs the question with a knock-down blow on the part of the captain, from which the boy staggers up—"sugar and spice and all things nice." That blow is no more explanatory than the rubbing of Aladdin's lamp; and thenceforward the story becomes part fairy-tale, part laborious, and mostly unconvincing realism; with a scented finish of sentimental snobbery—not to speak of the strong smell of codfish all the way through.

Now, we haven't waited for Mr. Kipling to hear about the heroism of the sea. There is a book of Victor Hugo's, at least. As against liners and millionnaires, our interests are entirely with cod-fishers. Only, you must make the cod-fishers as interesting as, say, Mr. Barrie has made his Scotch weavers. Mr. Kipling works very hard to do so, but nothing he does makes his men live. That he records the various processes of "cod" from catching to curing, leaves us cold. Any man on the New

York *Journal* could do that—much more imaginatively. All he does is to give us two or three pictures of the sea, beautiful pictures, one of which I will quote:

". . . since there was no fishing, Harvey had time to look at the sea from another point of view. The low-sided schooner was naturally on most intimate terms with her surroundings. They saw little of the horizon save when she topped a swell; and usually she was elbowing, fidgeting, and coaxing her steadfast way through gray, gray-blue, or black hollows laced across and across with streaks of shivering foam; or rubbing herself caressingly along the flank of some bigger water-hill. It was as if she said: 'You wouldn't hurt me, surely? I'm only the little *We're Here.*' Then she would slide away chuckling softly to herself till she was brought up by some fresh obstacle. The dullest of folk cannot see this kind of thing hour after hour through long days without noticing it; and

Harvey, being anything but dull, began to comprehend and enjoy the dry chorus of wave-tops turning over with a sound of incessant tearing; the hurry of the winds working across open spaces and herding the purple-blue cloud-shadows; the splendid upheaval of the red sunrise; the folding and packing away of the morning mists, wall after wall withdrawn across the white floors; the salty glare and blaze of noon; the kiss of rain falling over thousands of dead, flat square miles; the chilly blackening of everything at the day's end; and the million wrinkles of the sea under the moonlight, when the jib-boom solemnly poked at the low stars, and Harvey went down to get a doughnut from the cook."

But there has been worse than "Captains Courageous." In "The Day's Work," the title of which is a resolute text, Mr. Kipling has given intemperate rein to a boyish passion for machinery which we have all had once, or have seen possessing others. Anyone who knows anything of English seaports knows the boy who prides himself on knowing the particular flag, funnel, and tonnage of every vessel in the river. "It's the signal of the Cross Keys Line running to Australia. I wonder which steamer it is," said Dick Heldar proudly to Maisie. How one sympathises with his pride, for who has not known the boy who swelled with just that knowledge of forgotten steam-ship lore? Yet such lore, while it may be useful in a shipping office, is very rarely entertaining in general conversation; and must be used very sparingly indeed in literature. Mr. Kipling, however, has of late veritably debauched in it. To use an Americanism, he has just wallowed in technical terms, as a miser bathes himself in gold pieces. No engineer was ever so technical as Mr. Kipling. His technicalities would be more generalised, worn by use into pocket-slang. Let us take an example from "The Devil and the Deep Sea":

"The forward engine had no more work to do. Its released piston-rod, therefore, drove up fiercely, with nothing to check it, and started most of the nuts of the cylinder-cover. It came down again, the full weight of the steam behind it, and the foot of the disconnected connecting-rod, useless as the leg of a man with a sprained ankle, flung out to the right and struck the starboard, or right-hand, cast-iron supporting column of the forward engine, cracking it clean through about six inches above the base, and wedging the upper portion outwards three inches towards the ship's side. There the connecting-rod jammed. Meantime, the after engine, being as yet unembarrassed, went on with its work, and in so doing brought round at its next revolution the crank of the forward engine, which smote the already jammed connecting-rod, bending it and therewith the piston-rod cross-head—the big cross-piece that slides up and down so smoothly.

The cross-head jammed sideways in the guides, and, in addition to putting further pressure on the already broken starboard supporting column, cracked the port, or left-hand, supporting column in two or three places. There being nothing more that could be made to move, the engines brought up, all standing, with a hiccup that seemed to lift the *Haliotis* a foot out of the water; and the engine-room staff, opening every steam outlet that they could find in the confusion, arrived on deck somewhat scalded, but calm."

To write thus is as though a man should undertake to translate a Greek poem and leave three-quarters of it in Greek. This is certainly not the way to sing the song of steam.

It was just such an obsession of technical terminology that possessed Rabelais; but his terms were more universal. Walt Whitman's catalogues even are more justifiable, for they are more imaginatively characteristic in their particularity, and it must always be remembered, in criticising Whitman, that he, confessedly, aimed to suggest, rather than to sing, "the song of steam."

In "To be Filed for Reference" (the last story of "Plain Tales") Mr. Kipling, speaking of the Verlaine-like Englishman of learning whom he patronised and dowered with tobacco, says: ". . . he did most of his ravings in Greek or German. The man's mind was a perfect rag-bag of useless things." I venture to think that a "rag-bag" of Greek and German poets and philosophers would be a much more truly valuable tool-basket than those details of evanescent engineering which have covered so much of two recent pages. To be able to quote Horace is more important, from any broad human standpoint, than to be an initiate of the engine-room of the greatest liner afloat or to be floated.

As for "The Ship that Found Herself" or "·007," all that needs to be said of them is that they are exceedingly tedious Hans Andersen. "The Ship that Found Herself" has amusing touches and an excellent moral, but "·007" is, we shall hope, the *reductio ad absurdum* of Mr. Kipling's later method. His sympathy with all manufactured things is beautiful in itself. We all have that sympathy. We have not waited for him to realise that engineers and mechanics are heroes in their way. But it is one thing to realise a truth philosophically and another to embody it in literature. This Mr. Kipling has not done.

CHAPTER III

MR. KIPLING'S GENERAL SIGNIFICANCE AND INFLUENCE

Were Mr. Kipling to be considered as a writer of ballads and a teller of tales, and nothing besides, it had hardly seemed necessary to write a book about him; at all events, in the present stage of his career. Since the "Recessional," however, he has been definitely more than that; while, long before it, if less explicitly, he was no less virtually a national influence. His Indian stories and songs did just that service for the Imperialistic idea which the imaginative man can do. They made us realise, as we had never done before, what a great dependency like India means, and what it means to maintain it; and, by this extensive object-lesson, made us sensitive as never before of the organic relation between us and our possessions in the furthest seas. Mr. Kipling, so to speak, roused the sleeping nerve centres of Imperialism. So much we may gladly and gratefully admit, without, it is to be hoped, seeming to imply, as certain enthusiasts suffering from acute Kiplingitis do all but state, that Mr. Kipling is little short of the Saviour of the British Empire. Lovers of that beautiful phrase "Unification" really seem to think that all our Imperial sentries slept till Mr. Kipling blew his *réveillé* of Imperialism. But is it not one of the morals of Mr. Kipling's writings that the quiet, inglorious, strong men whom he nobly celebrates are at their posts as of old tirelessly watching? The men who won India may be trusted to keep it even without literary assistance.

A certain amount of jingoism was naturally—and properly—inseparable from such work as the "Barrack-Room Ballads" and the Indian tales. A certain amount of jingoism, or chauvinism, or what you will, is inseparable from national existence. A nation could hardly go on existing if it did not believe itself the finest nation on earth, and in England's case, it is obviously something more than a private opinion. But a nation may feel that, without falling into the old Jewish error of concluding that it is the chosen people of the Universe, and under the special care of the great Invisible powers,—particularly in the present era of thought. Ordinary jingoism may seem childish, but religious jingoism, nowadays, is something worse. Does Mr. Kipling literally believe that there is a Lord God of Hosts whom we please by our commercial conquests, and by whose favour victory sits upon our helms? If the answer is "Yes," it is difficult to see how it is to be reconciled with the prevalent cynicism and non-Christian tone of his writings. Besides, he has frankly professed himself a servant of "the God of things as they are," whom on one occasion he names as Dungara.

It may be said that the "Recessional" is symbolical, but, when using the terms of the Christian tradition for Englishmen, and in so momentous a connection, a poet has hardly more right to be symbolic than a clergyman in using those terms. Englishmen either don't understand, or are further strengthened in their natural hypocrisy; and the use of Christian terminology in England is sufficiently charged with hypocrisy without poets adding to it. Why not speak the truth? Conquests do not result from the exercise of the Christian virtues, but from their direct opposites; and, broadly speaking, the men who have made the British Empire may have been Christians in their private hours, but, while they did the public business, they were many very different things besides. Of course, faithfully speaking, there has never been a Christian nation, and never will be. A really Christian nation could not exist five minutes. In this matter of English conquests another living poet,* Mr. William Watson, has challenged the "Recessional" with unanswerable wit:

"Best by remembering God, say some,
  We keep our high imperial lot—
Fortune, I think, has mainly come,
  When we forgot—when we forgot."

To see how little Englishmen welcome the real Christian ideal in national poetry one has but to compare the reception of the "Recessional" and "The White Man's Burden" with the languid reception given to Mr. William Watson's noble Armenian sonnets. There was a white man's burden, if you like. There was a work to do on which the Lord God of Hosts had surely smiled. But no! we stood to lose in Ar-

* See "The Unknown God," in "The Collected Poems of William Watson."

menia. But we have no objection to taking up the white man's burden in the Soudan—where we stand to gain. Perhaps it must be admitted that interference in Armenia was too perilous for the general peace of the world for us to undertake. The earth cries out with sad, irremediable things, terrible cruelty and injustice, before which we can only wring our hands in utter helplessness. There is a frightful something in the working of the Universe, the operations of which we can but insignificantly stay. That nations as well as individuals—even strong "Christian" nations—must sometimes recognise this is obvious; but, having stayed our hand in Armenia, we must not talk of taking up the white man's burden till we can convince, say, France, that we have conquered the Soudan with the single-minded intention of benefiting the Soudanese. That it may be for the ultimate good of the Soudanese (if sufficient remain upon whom to form an average) is really beside the point of Christian jingoism. Like any other nation we conquer countries for the purely selfish and natural purpose of extending our trade. It is a natural law; but it is not a Christian proceeding, and we are the only Christian nation that pretends it is.

One is really inclined to believe that America took Cuba from Spain from something like Christian motives; and one may believe, too, that her annexation of the Philippines is a reluctant second move made necessary by the first. *She* has a certain right then, perhaps, to talk of taking up the white man's burden; but, presently, when the wealth of the Philippines begins to pour into the hands of American traders, America will begin to see (no doubt with innocent surprise) how small is the cost of taking up the white man's burden compared with the subsequent profit—and then it is to be feared she may hanker after more such burdens.

I have not meant to imply for a moment that Mr. Kipling is consciously insincere in his vein of sacred Imperialism. At the same time one must be allowed to criticise an attitude so at variance with the temper of the bulk of his work. Heretofore he has always been cynically, even brutally, realistic about the facts and methods of empire.

"Give 'em hell! Oh, give 'em hell!" cried Dick Heldar in ecstasy as the armoured train met the nightly attack of a few Soudanese on its way through the desert. And "give 'em hell" is the note of all the most typical Indian stories. Where, for example, in that vivid picture of a butcher's shop called "The Drums of the Fore and Aft" is there a hint of pity for the Afghan—"half savage and half child"? What is he but so much butcher's meat for the noble British soldier to hack and hew, "to a nasty noise as of beef being cut on a block"? The scoundrel to resist our invasion of his mountain homes! Not a hint of any civilised feeling for a noble race inevitably breaking, not before superior courage or physique, but merely superior cleverness and better machines. True, "he's a first-class fighting man." But that's all. Such is Tommy's simple view, and Mr. Kipling's is no less simple. Tommy's is sheer primitive ignorance, Mr. Kipling's is—what?

It may be, of course, that Mr. Kipling begins to repent of his sins of blood; but if we are to take his new doctrine seriously we must first see him advocating other methods of conquest. "Give 'em hell! Oh, give 'em hell!" and "The White Man's Burden" are utterances that cannot go on being made side by side, without justifiable suspicions of cant, though, perhaps, another reason may be suggested, possibly the right one.

I have hinted elsewhere at a vein of sentimentality which runs throughout Mr.

Kipling's work, curiously parallel with its uncompromising realism, and analogous to the vein of fantastic farce even more evident. In the story we have just referred to, the horrible cynicism of the battle picture is suddenly contrasted with as flagrant a piece of drummer-boy sentimentality as was ever perpetrated. The thing is half Kipling and half John Strange Winter. It is none the worse for that, except that the two halves don't join, and while Mr. Kipling's makes us believe all about the bloodshed, he does not make us believe in his drummer-boys. The one half is his own, the other half is a clever *pastiche* in another method which doesn't come so natural to him. One has the "blood and tobacco" reality which Maisie complained of in Dick Heldar's picture; the other reminds one of the nice, clean, pipe-clayed soldier, with shiny boots, which Dick Heldar painted in an ironical fit to please the British public. Many such contrasts of reality and fairy-tale sentimentality may be found in Mr. Kipling's writings, but this will suffice.

Now I think the same thing takes place at times in his thought. On one side he is a sad-hearted pessimist, much given to that "cold rage" that

> "seizes one at whiles
> To show the bitter old and wrinkled truth,"

—and one may note his fondness for quoting James Thomson—on the other he reveals a strong vein of religious mysticism, now and again finding beautiful convincing expression, but at others degenerating into the clap-trap mysticism of such poems as the dedication to Wolcott Balestier before mentioned, and into a religious sentimentalism which we may, not impertinently, trace to the Wesleyanism known to be in his blood.

It is quite possible for a man to believe two or more different things at once, or to think he believes them—which is about as deep as the roots of belief really go. He may, perhaps, give expression to the two or more beliefs side by side, without any insincerity. It is impossible, however, that the value of his utterances should not be diminished; and in spite of their great popular reception, and of their use politically, the "Recessional" and "The White Man's Burden" mark not an increase, but a decrease of Mr. Kipling's real authority. They are reactionary in the direction of sentimental superstition, and, however sincerely Mr. Kipling meant them, are serious reinforcements of British national hypocrisy.

But, of course, Mr. Kipling is nothing if not reactionary. If, on the one hand, he belongs to the age that invented the cinematograph and discovered the Röntgen rays, he is no less a product of the age that has produced the Dreyfus Case; an age that has looked on cold-eyed at the massacre of the Armenians and the suppression of the Finns; an age that is to see the re-opening of a bull-ring at Havre, a bull-ring, one reads, which is mainly to rely for its support on English visitors—one of the most unscrupulous ages of the world. At the present moment, as I have before had occasion to remark, in England—in fact, all over the world—the things of the mind are at a discount. There is in England just now a public opinion corresponding in no small degree to the present contempt in France for the "intellectuels"; that is, for those who regard human life as something more than brute force, brutal rivalries, and brutal pleasures. We are in the thick of one of the most cynically impudent triumphs of the Philistines the world has seen. All that should be meant by civilisation is a mock. The once kindly fields of literature are beneath the heels of a set of literary rough-riders. All the nobler and gentler instincts of men and women are ridiculed as sentimentality. All the hard-won gains of nineteenth-century philosophers are thrown to the winds; and for the minor ameliorations of science we have to pay with the most diabolical development of the foul art of war. Everywhere the brute and the bully—and for the ape and tiger truly a glorious resurrection!

For this state of things in England Mr. Kipling is the most responsible voice. Of course, he did not create it. Such tidal moods of mankind go deeper than the influence of single personalities; or, indeed, if such cause them, they are usually long since dead, and the final effect springs from the cumulative power of their influence. Mr. Kipling's is not a lonely voice crying to-day what all will feel to-morrow. He is the voice of the tide at its height. Yet if the mood creates the voice, the voice powerfully reinforces the mood. There is a captaincy in expression, and such is the responsibility of the voice. And, at all events, if the voice has no real responsibility, one is obliged to treat it as though it had. Mr. Kipling stands for a certain view of life which some regret, and, as spokesman, is responsible for that view.

More than any other writer he has given expression to the physical force ideal at present fashionable, and the brutality inseparable from that ideal.

How far indeed have we wandered from the spirit of lines such as these:

> "Have you numbered all the birds of the wood,
> Without a gun?
> Have you loved the wild rose—
> And left it on its stalk?
> O be my friend, and teach me to be thine"—

wandered so far, indeed, that the very expression of it, though it be that of a great spiritual teacher, will, no doubt, to some appear silly in its gentleness.

One may recall Mr. Kipling's "On Greenhow Hill" as a contrast. A native deserter had been troubling the camp at nights, and doubtless it was necessary that he should be caught and shot. However, entirely without instructions, Ortheris makes it known to his two friends that the game is to be his, and invites them to spend the day with him over against a valley along which every afternoon the deserter is known to make his way towards the camp. It is to be a sort of picnic, and meanwhile Mulvaney will oblige with a tale, or, as it proves on this occasion, Learoyd, while the three lie under cover, Ortheris fondling his rifle, and always with his eye on the valley. With beer and pipes added, the little shooting party spend a pleasant afternoon waiting for Ortheris's game. As the story ends, the story of Learoyd's heart:

"Ortheris suddenly rose to his knees, his rifle at his shoulder, and peered across the valley in the clear afternoon light. His chin cuddled the stock, and there was a twitching of the muscles of the right cheek as he sighted; Private Stanley Ortheris was engaged on his business. A speck of white crawled up the watercourse.

" 'See that beggar? . . . Got 'im.'

"Seven hundred yards away, and a full two hundred down the hillside, the deserter of the Aurangabadis pitched forward, rolled down a red rock, and lay very still, with his face in a clump of blue gentians, while a big raven flapped out of the pinewood to make investigation.

" 'That's a clean shot, little man,' said Mulvaney.

"Learoyd thoughtfully watched the smoke clear away.

" 'Happen there was a lass tewed up wi' him, too,' said he.

"Ortheris did not reply. He was staring across the valley, with the smile of the artist who looks on the completed work."

Now one understands that deserters have got to be shot, and that soldiers have no time to faint at the sight of blood, or shed tears upon their fallen foes. War is war, and among its hideous necessities is the making of men like Ortheris. That is understood. But it is one thing to accept a hideous fact, and another to glorify it. Though in this story Mr. Kipling makes no overt comment, presenting the picture simply and nakedly as a piece of life, there has yet crept into the telling, as in all his stories of the kind, a certain tone of approval, even gusto, which leaves one in little doubt of his own feeling. It is murder as one of the fine arts, and the victim is—hardly a dog. And if he does not exactly glorify this particular example, he certainly has done his best to glorify the barbarous system in which it is but a minor episode. He is unmistakably the drum and fife in modern literature.

The plain truth about Ortheris, as revealed to us in this story, is that, whatever admirable qualities he possesses, and allowing that the blame is less his than the conditions that made him, he is simply a criminal with a gun license. His profession gives him the opportunity, in the name of fighting for his country, and protected by other such glittering euphemisms, to gratify that lust of murder which lies not too far below the surface in all human beings. He enjoyed killing that wretched native, as a sportsman enjoys bringing down a partridge. He was a little angry with the man because, as he put it, his "beauty-sleep" had been destroyed by the nightly disturbances, but so the thing became a trifle more pleasurable. Civilians are only allowed to shoot pheasants and such small game, and those under expensive restrictions,

> "But for pleasure and profit together,
> Allow me the hunting of Man."

Such is the Tommy Atkins whom Mr.

Kipling has chosen for his hero, and a rather superior example, one gathers, from his creator's evident affection for him.

That his hero's taste for murder is not unsympathetic to Mr. Kipling, one is hardly left in doubt by one or two other of the stories. Take, for instance, the story in which Ortheris, again the hero, is struck on parade by a nervous young officer. Mr. Kipling represents himself as watching the whole thing from the glacis of the fort, and he sympathetically explains how the young officer came to do it. He was new to his work; had not yet learned to give his commands with confidence, and, hot and flustered with the stupidity of the raw men he was drilling—a batch of recruits with a sprinkling of old hands amongst them—he had struck the nearest man lightly with his cane. The man chanced to be one of the old hands—Ortheris. The captain, happening to go by, had seen the thing, and the young officer is about to betray himself, when Ortheris salutes, and tells the captain a cock-and-bull story to save his officer. In fact, he behaves like a brick.

But it is to Mr. Kipling's own comment that I wish to draw attention. "If Ortheris," he says, "had slipped in a cartridge and cleared the account at once I should have rejoiced!"

I should have *rejoiced.* There is no mistake about the verb. And this is not Tommy Atkins. It is Mr. Kipling in his own person. Had Ortheris, for an offence which Mr. Kipling, at all events, clearly saw to be a slip of nervous petulance, taken his officer's life, Mr. Kipling would have *rejoiced.*

But the story which leaves no doubt as to Mr. Kipling's genuine, unaffected love of brutality is "The Light that Failed." We are not justified in regarding Dick Heldar as entirely autobiographical; but there can be no fair denial that he is so in certain particulars important in our present connection. He was a war correspondent in love with soldiers. "O my men, my beautiful men!" he cries, as in his blindness he hears the soldiers pass in Hyde Park. After some years of adventure and campaign his pictures from the Soudan suddenly "catch on," and he goes to London, to find himself a famous man. There he meets with a great deal of talk about "Art," on which he expresses himself much after the fashion of Mr. Kipling. He has loads of tenderness underneath, but his manners, as those of his fellow war artists and correspondents, are as truculently masculine as all known methods can make them. He loves nobly and once for all, and is rewarded with a coldness which, under the final circumstances, becomes quite inhuman. Yet he never utters a word of complaint. The stoicism, which is one of Mr. Kipling's *good* lessons, supports him. And, great as is his love for Maisie, there is just a hinted doubt whether his love for "the old hot, unregenerate life is not stronger." Even before his blindness, on his one comparatively happy day with Maisie, the "go-fever" came strong upon him with the sight of the sea. The reader can hardly be blamed then for thinking that in many essential respects Dick Heldar and Rudyard Kipling are one.

Well, remembering that, recall again the scene when Heldar, blind, and hopeless of his love, returns to the Soudan determined on the one thing left him—to die among the spears. Just one smell of the old life he could no longer see, and then to go out for ever. The journey, full of muffled recognitions of the old life, is terrible in its tragedy; but as it nears its end, one almost loses the tragedy in the horrible glee with which the mere darkened nearness to slaughter fills the blind man.

"'Listen!' said Dick. A flight of heavy-handed bullets was succeeded by yelling and shouts. The children of the desert valued their nightly amusement, and the train was an excellent mark.

"'Is it worth while giving them half a hopper full?' the subaltern asked of the engine which was driven by a Lieutenant of Sappers.

"'I should just think so! This is my section of the line. They'll be playing old Harry with my permanent way if we don't stop 'em.'

"'Right O!'

"'*Hrrmph!*' said the machine gun through all its five noses as the subaltern drew the lever home. The empty cartridges clashed on the floor and the smoke blew back through the truck. There were indiscriminate firing at the rear of the train, a return fire from the darkness without and unlimited howling. Dick stretched himself on the floor, wild with delight at the sounds and the smells.

"'God is very good—I never thought

I'd hear this again. Give 'em hell, men! Oh, give 'em hell!' he cried."

This is the bellowing of mere homicidal lust. It is not the fine battle rapture which, under certain inspiring conditions, one can understand. It is the sheer glee of the slaying of men—or rather of hearing them slain. It is an even less restrained exhibition of murderous passion than Ortheris's exhibition of artistry. It is the mere delight in the smell of blood. It is blood-madness. But war correspondents, like soldiers, are nowadays allowed a certain blood-madness, and the alacrity with which they hasten to indulge their privilege on the first whisper of a war is but another sign of that renaissance of cruelty which is characteristic of the time.

I am not writing from the point of view of one who has no knowledge of such feelings. That it would be difficult to do, for there are few of us, I fear, who have not something, indeed a good deal, somewhere in us that gloatingly responds to cruelty and bloodshed. But, remembering that it has taken all these centuries even to chain, not to speak of taming, that beast in us; remembering the agonies of human history for which it has been responsible; remembering, too, how ever ready it is to snap the all too slight chain of civilisation: surely his is an evil service to humanity who shall in any way help to set loose again so terrible a monster as human cruelty. And that is what it means to glorify war.

Who, knowing what war is—and none knows better than Mr. Kipling—shall deliberately glorify war, horrible always, but ten times more horrible to-day, however brilliantly, humourously, persuasively he does it, is an enemy of society; and the more brilliantly he does it, the greater is his crime.

Mr. Kipling not only glorifies war, but he is never tired of hinting his poor opinion of the stay-at-home man of peace who cannot take murder in his light and airy fashion, and for whom death retains some of its pity and solemnity. What good fun he makes out of the distinguished novelist talking with three young officers home from India, and realising, bit by bit, what their profession means!

"'You! Have you shot a man? . . . And have *you* too?'

"'Think so,' said Nevin sweetly.

"'Good heavens! And how did you feel afterwards?'

"'Thirsty. I wanted a smoke too.'"

How fine to be able to feel—or rather not to feel—like that; and what charming taste in the expression of that heroic nonchalance! No wonder the great novelist felt himself a poor milksop "intellectuel" in the presence of these noble boys; for, as Mulvaney has said, "Canteen baccy's like the Army. It shpoils a man's taste for milder things."

And what a fine contempt is Mr. Kipling's for the young recruit, who, as yet unused to bloodshed, turns white in his first action, and "grows acutely miserable when he hears a comrade turn over with the rattle of fire-irons falling into the fender, and the grunt of a pole-axed ox"! Perhaps no one ever wrote so profanely of death as Mr. Kipling, or with such heartless vulgarity.

But one has only to read the newspaper headlines to realise that in this respect, too, Mr. Kipling is the child, as well as the voice, of the moment. A railway accident is now a "smash," a fatal fire is a "big blaze," and, of course, such are only indicative straws. Whatever the reason may be, there is unmistakably at the moment a general indifference to human suffering, and in some quarters a marked revival of interest in brutality. And one encounters it more often, perhaps, among women than men. The Roman lady of the gladiatorial shows is by no means uncommon in English society at the moment.

The Englishman has always been a strange combination of gentleman and brute. The gentleman has been besung to weariness. In Mr. Kipling we have him too; but for the most part Mr. Kipling's work is an appeal to, and a vindication of, the Englishman as brute. The Englishman, too, as Philistine. That particular Englishman has had rather a dull time of it, in regard to literature, for the past fifty years. In fact, Victorian literature has been painfully spiritual and intellectual. It has gone in for problems and making the world better, for solving "the riddle," and keeping down the ape and tiger. Between Ruskin societies, and Browning societies, and pre-Raphaelite poetry (not to speak of those terrible Burne-Jones women) what wonder if the young Englishman has not yawned and longed to go out and shoot something he could understand! However, being exceedingly docile and, despite his physical courage, of small moral courage, he has gone on submitting to his sisters in these matters. For there was not a single writer of genius to take his part. Then came Stevenson, with his books of adventure, and his gospel of manliness; and the young Englishman began to hope. But then Stevenson was far from brutal enough. Then, too, he had a style. Fatal disadvantage. It gets in the way so.

Then at last came Mr. Kipling, and the young Englishman had the permission of a man of undoubted genius to be just as brutal as he liked. The thing was as true to life as the cinematograph of a prize-fight, and everyone said it was genius too. He had waited a long while for it, but at last it came, a complete Triumph of the Philistines. And now the literature of beauty, of thought, of fancy, all the literature of idealism, can go pack. It must subscribe to the new fashion, or die. All the old literary ideals must be discarded even by the literary journals. Idealism flies in panic; or bows down, abjectly sacrificing in terror one reputation after another before the conqueror. The old masters were milksops and knew nothing about writing whatsoever. Literary oracles in New York declare that Mr. Kipling is the greatest master of English prose that has ever written, and an authoritative English journal timidly suggests that there may be one or two of the higher notes of poetry in which Tennyson is Mr. Kipling's superior. But you feel that the editor has taken his life in his hands. Wilder and wilder grows the popular taste for blood. "More chops," goes up the cry more fiercely every hour, "more chops, bloody ones with gristle." No one writer can keep pace with the gruesome demand for blood-stained fiction, and so a vast school of battle-and-murder novelists arises, with horses and carriages and country seats and much-photographed babies; and ever the cry goes up, growing to a veritable roar: "More chops, can't you! Bloody ones with gristle."

No doubt there is an element of fantastic generalisation in this statement of the situation; but, broadly speaking, it is true of the main current of popular taste. Perhaps we need not seek far for the reason of this widespread reversion to brutality and sensationalism in literature. Is it not the revulsion of an age sick at heart with much thinking; a pessimistic age that is tired to death with the riddle of things; an age that has lost one faith and not yet found another? an age, therefore, that sees but one immediate resource: to take its material pleasures, ruthlessly if need be, and in the coarse excitements life offers to silence the pangs of thought.

For all the humour and buoyancy of his writings Mr. Kipling is at heart a pessimist, and, perhaps, his sincerest expression of opinion in regard to the government of the universe is contained in the fierce Omarian exclamation of Holden in "Without Benefit of Clergy," addressed to no one in particular, but evidently meant to reach far up into the skies: "O you brute! You utter brute!" So Omar bade Allah "man's forgiveness give and take."

One often sees Mr. Kipling praised as being startlingly "modern." It is true that he is—remarkably contemporary. Contemporaneousness he carries to the point of genius. But modern, in the larger sense of the term, he is not. In fact, of all European writers of importance to-day he is least modern. True, he is modern in that pessimism to which I have just referred; but of modern hope and modern endeavour he knows nothing or has nothing good to say. For typically modern movements he has nothing but cynical or good-humoured contempt. Democracy, the woman-movement, the education of the masses; these are favourite butts of his laughter, and "the Refining Influence of Civilisation and the March of Progress" one of his favourite sneers. Wiser men have dreamed of a gradual *rapprochement* of the nations, a dwindling of meaningless race-hatreds, even an ultimate union of separate peoples, for the general good of mankind. His influence, however, is all on the side of a narrow patriotism that can see no nation but its own, and against a nation so near to us in blood as America he is not above directing the antiquated sneer.

His work nobly enforces those old-fashioned virtues of man which, it is to be hoped, will never go out of fashion—to do one's duty, to live stoically, to live cleanly, to live cheerfully. Such lessons can never be taught too often, and they are of the moral bone and fibre of Mr. Kipling's writing. But with them go all the old-fashioned vices of prejudiced Toryism. For progressive thought there has been no such dangerous influence in England for many years. Of all that our best poets, philosophers, and social economists have been working for he is directly, or indirectly, a powerful enemy. For is he not, on his own admission, a servant of "the great God Dungara, the God of Things as They Are, Most Terrible, One-eyed, Bearing the Red Elephant Tusk"? A god, indeed, not unlike the Jehovah of the "Recessional," but very different from the gentle meliorist to whom the so-called Christian nation of England professes a hollow allegiance. Of one melioristic movement only he seems to be the friend: the crusade against drink.

It is Mr. Kipling and his followers who are the true end-of-the-century *decadents*, for it would seem to be their aim to begin the twentieth century by throwing behind them all that the nineteenth century has so painfully won.

I have in these pages paid my tribute to Mr. Kipling's great gifts; paid it, I trust, with something of that generosity which beseems one of the many thousands whom he has so generously delighted. If there was nothing else to be grateful for, he is the one real humourist vouchsafed to England for some years. His farce alone is a well of precious laughter. Then it is painful to have had to write hard things of the man who made "Mandalay," and gave us the "Jungle Books." His mere vitality, apart from the variousness of it, is a joy to contemplate. Yet all these good reasons for praise are equally good reasons for fear, when we find gifts so remarkable wedded to a point of view hardly less advanced than that of the British soldier they have so handsomely celebrated.

As a writer Mr. Kipling is a delight; as an influence he is a danger. Of course, the clock of Time is not to be set back by gifts ten times as great as Mr. Kipling's. The great world movement will still go on, moving surely, if slowly, and with occasional relapses, in the direction which it has always taken, from brute force to spiritual enlargement. But there are influences that speed it along and others that retard. It is to be regretted that Mr. Kipling's influence should be one of those that retard.

RUDYARD KIPLING
A BIBLIOGRAPHY
(1881—1899)

BY

JOHN LANE

INTRODUCTORY NOTE

It is difficult to conceive of anything more exciting to the true bibliographer than Kiplingana. Mr. Kipling's juvenilia were numerous and interesting; from the contributions to his school magazine, which he edited (hence perhaps his recent good-natured contribution to the *Horsmonden Budget*), to the privately-printed opuscula of his family and himself. Parallels occur in the productions of the juvenile Rossettis, from the Polidori Press; and the youthful productions of Robert Louis Stevenson. We do not learn that Mr. Kipling made illustrations or decorations for his own booklets, but then, of course, he had a master of design in his father, Mr. J. Lockwood Kipling, whose care for the externals of his son's work, begun so early, has lasted up to the magnificent collected edition; and this devotion to one another of father and son is one of the most beautiful features in modern literary annals. The bibliographer has much sport in finding out the whys and wherefores of the first editions of the Indian Railway Library.

No doubt errors will be discovered in the following pages, and I shall gladly welcome any information that will enable me to correct them, in the event of further editions being called for.

It is possible that Mr. Kipling may not be gratified at my drawing attention to portions of his works not yet reprinted; but that his admirers will thank me I have very little doubt.

My thanks are specially due to Col. W. F. Prideaux, whose aid has been invaluable; also to Mr. W. J. Dare, Mr. Frederic Denham, Mr. H. J. Brown, Mr. Robson, Mr. Thomas Hodge, Mr. Lionel Jones, and to my friend Mr. Herbert G. Jenkins, without whose assistance the work could not have been carried through.

JOHN LANE.

G1, The Albany, Piccadilly, W.
October 7th, 1899.

A BIBLIOGRAPHY OF RUDYARD KIPLING.

1881—1894.

THE UNITED SERVICES COLLEGE CHRONICLE. Published as the College Magazine at "Westward Ho," Northam, North Devon, where Rudyard Kipling was educated. He was co-editor from June, 1881, to December, 1882 (Nos. 4 to 12 inclusive), and a contributor at intervals until the year 1894.

1881.

"(*Printed for private circulation only.*)"

SCHOOLBOY LYRICS. | BY | RUDYARD KIPLING. | Lahore. | Printed at the "Civil and Military Gazette" Press | 1881. | Fcap. 8vo. (in many cases cut down), pp. iv, unnumbered, and 46 Brown paper wrapper, with title and author's name in centre, a repetition of title page.

1884.

ECHOES. | BY TWO WRITERS. |

The Duke: "A new Song, Sirrah?"
1st Minstrel: "New as new bread,
Baked with the corn of yester year, my lord:

The fledglings of the nest will try their pipes,
And shrill it boldly in the same old tunes
You hear on every woodland bough."

Old Play.

Medium 16mo., pp iv. (second page of contents numbered ii.), and 72 N D [1884] Light buff wrapper, with "Echoes | By Two Writers" running diagonally from bottom left-hand corner, and "Lahore: The Civil and Military Gazette Press" horizontally at foot.

1885.

1885 | QUARTETTE. | The Christmas Annual | of the | Civil & Military Gazette | BY | FOUR ANGLO-INDIAN WRITERS. | Lahore: | The "Civil and Military Gazette" Press | MDCCCLXXXV. Royal 8vo. (cut down) pp. iv., unnumbered, and 125, also viii. pp. of advertisements, numbered, at end. Grey paper wrappers.

"The Strange Ride" of Morrowbie Jukes" and "The Phantom 'Rickshaw" first appeared in this publication.

The "Four Anglo-Indians" were Mr. and Mrs. J. Lockwood Kipling and their Son and Daughter.

1886.

DEPARTMENTAL | DITTIES | AND OTHER | VERSES. | No. I. of 1886. On Her Majesty's Service Only. | To | All Heads of Departments | and All Anglo-Indians. | RUDYARD KIPLING, Assistant. | Department of Public Journalism | Lahore District. Oblong 8vo., pp. vi., unnumbered, and 56, unnumbered. Printed on one side only. Buff paper wrapper, in form of a public document, with flap, upon which, in the form of a circular seal, appears: Lahore | The Civil | and | Military | Gazette | Press. |

Third Edition. Crown 8vo. (broad), pp. viii., numbered, and 84. Blue cloth. Calcutta: Thacker, Spink, & Co. London: W. Thacker & Co. 1888.

Fourth Edition, with Additional Poems. Pp. viii., numbered, and 121. Green cloth. Calcutta: Thacker, Spink, & Co. London: W. Thacker & Co. Bombay: Thacker & Co., Ltd. 1890.

Fifth Edition. Pp. viii., numbered, and 121. Blue cloth. Calcutta: Thacker, Spink and Co. London: W. Thacker and Co. Bombay: Thacker & Co., Ltd. 1890.

Sixth Edition. Pp. viii., unnumbered, and 125. Blue cloth. This edition has a Glossary added; in other respects it is identical with the Fifth Edition. 1891.

Ninth Edition (Japanese vellum), with Illustrations by Dudley Cleaver. 8vo., pp. 189. Bound ¼ parchment, blue linen sides, with design in gold. 1898.

Tenth Edition, with Illustrations by Dudley Cleaver. Pp. xvi., numbered, and 189. London: Thacker and Co. 1898.

A Cheap Edition. Demy 8vo., pp. 126, paper wrapper. Portrait. Geo. Newnes & Co., Ltd. 1899.

1888.

PLAIN TALES | FROM | THE HILLS | BY | RUDYARD KIPLING | Author of "Departmental Ditties and other Verses." | Calcutta: | Thacker, Spink & Co. | London: | W. Thacker & Co. | 1888. Crown 8vo., pp. xii., numbered. and 283, verso of last page blank. Bound in citron cloth. 28 of the 40 tales appeared originally in the "Civil and Military Gazette," the others were new. Contents: "Lispeth," "Three and—an Extra," "Thrown Away," "Miss Youghal's Sais," "Yoked with an Unbeliever," "False Dawn," "The Rescue of Pluffles," "Cupid's Arrows," "The Three Musketeers," "His Chance of Life," "Watches of the Night," "The Other Man," "Consequences," "The Conversion of Aurelian McGoggin," "The Taking of Lungtungpen," "A Germ Destroyer," "Kidnapped," "The Arrest of Lieutenant Golightly," "In the House of Suddhoo," "His Wedded Wife," "The Broken-link Handicap," "Beyond the Pale," "In Error," "A Bank Fraud," "Tod's Amendment," "The Daughter of the Regiment," "In the Pride of His Youth," "Pig," "The Rout of the White Hussars," "The Bronckhorst Divorce-Case," "Venus Annodomini," "The Bisara of Pooree," "A Friend's Friend," "The Gate of the Hundred Sorrows," "The Madness of Private Ortheris," "The Story of Muhammad Din," "On the Strength of a Likeness," "Wressley of the Foreign Office," "By Word of Mouth," "To be Filed for Reference."

Third Edition. Pp. x., numbered, and 310. Blue cloth. Macmillan & Co., London. 1890.

SOLDIERS THREE | A COLLECTION OF STORIES | Setting forth certain Passages in the Lives and | Adventures of Privates Terence Mulvaney, | Stanley Ortheris, and John Learoyd, | Done into type and Edited by | RUDYARD KIPLING. | "We be Soldiers Three— | *Pardonnez moy, je vous en prie.*" | Allahabad: | Printed at the "Pioneer" Press | 1888. 12mo., pp. viii., unnumbered, and 97, verso of last page blank, L'Envoi, verso blank, and advertisements vi. pp., numbered. Green-grey paper wrapper, with lithographed design on front and back by J. Lockwood Kipling, "No. I. A. H. Wheeler & Co.'s Indian Railway Library. One Rupee." Contents: "The God from the Machine," "Private Learoyd's Story," "The Big Drunk Draf'," "The Solid Muldoon," "With the Main Guard," "In the Matter of a Private," "Black Jack."

First English and later Editions vary slightly from above. Pp. viii., unnumbered, and 94. London: Sampson Low. 1890.

THE | STORY OF THE GADSBYS, | A TALE WITHOUT A PLOT. | BY | RUDYARD KIPLING | Published by | Messrs. A. H. Wheeler & Co. | Allahabad. | N.D., [1888]. 12mo., ii. pp. advertisements, pp. vi., numbered, and 100, L'Envoi, verso blank, advertisements, viii. pp., numbered. Green-grey paper wrapper, with a lithographed design on front and back by J. Lockwood Kipling. "No. II. of A. H. Wheeler & Co.'s Indian Railway Library. One Rupee." Contents: "Poor Dear Mamma," "The World Without," "The Tents of Kedar," "With Any Amazement," "The Garden of Eden," "Fatima," "The Valley of the Shadow," "The Swelling of Jordan."

First English and later Edition varies slightly from above. Pp. vi., numbered, and 94. London: Sampson Low. 1890.

IN BLACK & WHITE. | BY | RUDYARD KIPLING. | Published by | Messrs. A. H. Wheeler & Co., | Allahabad. | N.D., [1888.] 12mo., ii. pp. advertisements, pp. viii., numbered, and 106, dedication ii. pp., numbered, advertisements viii. pp., numbered. White paper wrappers, with a lithographed design on front and back by J. Lockwood Kipling. "No. III. of A. H. Wheeler & Co.'s Indian Railway Library. One Rupee." Contents: "Dray Wara Yow Dee," "The Judgment of Dungara," "At Howli Thana," "Gemini," "At Twenty-Two," "In Flood Time," "The Sending of Dana Da," "On the City Wall."

First English and later Editions vary slightly from above. Pp. vi., numbered, and 96. London: Sampson Low. 1890.

UNDER THE DEODARS. | BY | RUDYARD KIPLING. |

And since he cannot spend nor use aright
  The little time here given him in trust,
But wasteth it in weary undelight
  Of foolish toil and trouble, strife and lust,
He naturally clamours to inherit
The Everlasting Future that his merit
  May have full scope—as surely is most just.
The City of Dreadful Night.

Published by | Messrs. A. H. Wheeler & Co., Allahabad. | N.D. [1888]. 12mo., ii. pp. advertisements, pp. vi., and 106, advertisements viii. pp., numbered. Green-grey paper wrapper, with a lithographed design on front and back by J. Lockwood Kipling. "No. IV. of Wheeler & Co.'s Indian Railway Library. One Rupee." Contents: "The Education of Otis Yeere," "At the Pit's Mouth," "A Wayside Comedy," "The Hill of Illusion," "A Second-Rate Woman." "Only a Subaltern."

First English and later Editions vary slightly from above. Pp. vi., unnumbered, and 96. London: Sampson Low. 1890.

THE PHANTOM 'RICKSHAW | AND OTHER TALES. | BY | RUDYARD KIPLING. | Published by | Messrs. A. H. Wheeler & Co. | Allahabad | N.D. [1888]. 12mo., ii. pp. advertisements, pp. vi., and 114, advertisements viii. pp., numbered. Green-grey paper wrapper, with a lithographed design on front and back by J. Lockwood Kipling. "No. V. of Wheeler & Co.'s Indian Railway Library. One Rupee." Contents: "The Phantom 'Rickshaw," "My Own True Ghost Story," "The Strange Ride of Morrowbie Jukes," "The Man who would be King."

First English and later Editions vary slightly from above. Pp. vi., unnumbered, and 104. London: Sampson Low. 1890.

WEE WILLIE WINKIE | AND OTHER CHILD STORIES. | BY | RUDYARD KIPLING. | Published by | Messrs. A. H. Wheeler & Co. | Allahabad. | N.D. [1888.] 12mo., ii. pp. advertisements, unnumbered, pp. vi. and 104, advertisements vii. pp., numbered. Green-grey paper wrappers. "No. VI. of A. & H. Wheeler's Indian Railway Library. One Rupee." Contents: "Wee Willie Winkie," "Baa, Baa, Black Sheep," "His Majesty, the King," "The Drums of the Fore and Aft."

First English and later Editions vary slightly from above. Pp. vi., unnumbered, and 96. London: Sampson Low. 1890.

1890.

THE COURTING OF DINAH SHADD | AND OTHER STORIES. | BY | RUDYARD KIPLING, | Author of "Plain Tales from the Hills," etc. | with | a Biographical and Critical Sketch | By ANDREW LANG. | (Monogram) New York | Harper & Brothers, Franklin Square | 1890. Imp. 16mo., pp. xii. and 182. (Portrait facing title.) Light blue paper wrapper. Contents: "Biographical Sketch of Rudyard Kipling," "The Courting of Dinah Shadd," "The Man Who Was," "A Conference of the Powers," "Without Benefit of Clergy," "On Greenhow Hill," "The Incarnation of Krishna Mulvaney." The first five stories originally appeared in "Harper's Weekly." All of them, with the exception of "A Conference of the Powers" ("Many Inventions"), were republished in "Life's Handicap" (Macmillan & Co., 1891), in America, and, with the exception of "A Conference of the Powers" (United Service Magazine), all appeared in Macmillan's Magazine in England.

THE | CITY OF DREADFUL NIGHT | AND | OTHER SKETCHES | BY | RUDYARD KIPLING | A. H. Wheeler & Co. | Allahabad. | 1890 | All rights reserved. 12mo. Brown cloth. Bearing the following inscription on fly leaf in writing of E. W. Buckeley:

"Of this book an edition of 3000 copies printed for Wheeler & Co. was cancelled. A new volume bearing the same title was subsequently issued by the Pioneer Press, but containing different matter to that found in this volume of the cancelled edition, and three copies only were preserved.

(*Signed*) "E. W. BUCKELEY,

"*General Manager.*

"Pioneer Press

"Allahabad,

"Sept., 1890."

This edition contained the seven articles on Calcutta under the heading of "The City of Dreadful Night," as they appeared in later editions, with the addition of eleven stories not reprinted.

1891.

THE | SMITH ADMINISTRATION | BY | RUDYARD KIPLING. | A. H. Wheeler & Co., | Allahabad. | 1891 | [All Rights Reserved] Extra Crown 8vo., pp ii, unnumbered, and 92. Bound in brown cloth boards, lettered in gold, top right-hand corner, "Smith Administration | Kipling." On right-hand page of first end-paper appears, in the writing of E. W. Buckeley:

"Of this book an edition of 3000 copies were printed and bound ready for sale for Messrs. Wheeler & Co., Allahabad, but owing to a difference of opinion as to copyrights between Rudyard Kipling and the Proprietors of the "Pioneer" and "Civil and Military Gazette" (in which journals the stories first appeared) the complete edition was cancelled and destroyed with the exception of three copies.

(*Signed*) "E. W. BUCKELEY,
"*General Manager*.

"Pioneer Press, Allahabad,
"1894.
"No. 2."

The foregoing, I have been able to gather, is correct, save that instead of 3000 copies, *three* only were printed and bound for the purpose of obtaining orders, and eventually the type was distributed without any further impressions being taken. I have received indisputable information upon this matter, the correctness of which is borne out by the fact that no numbers appear against the various stories in the list of "contents," although the spaces are there, headed with the word "page."

THE | CITY OF DREADFUL NIGHT | AND | OTHER PLACES | DEPICTED | BY | RUDYARD KIPLING. | A. H. Wheeler & Co. | Allahabad. | 1891 | [All Rights Reserved.] 12mo., iv. pp. advertisements, unnumbered, pp. iv., and 108. On page 108: "Printed at the 'Pioneer' Press, Allahabad." Advertisements x. pp. Green-grey paper wrapper, with a lithographed design on front and back by J. Lockwood Kipling. "No. 14 of Wheeler & Co.'s Indian Railway Library. One Rupee." Contents: "The City of Dreadful Night," "Among the Railway Folk," "The Giridih Coal Fields," "In an Opium Factory."

This work has also, as far as possible, been suppressed by Mr. Kipling.

The First English and later Editions vary slightly from above. Pp. ii., unnumbered, and 96. London: Sampson Low.

AMERICAN SERIES | AMERICAN NOTES | BY | RUDYARD KIPLING, Author of "Soldiers Three," "Plain Tales from the Hills," | "The Story of the Gadsbys," "The Phantom 'Rickshaw," | "The Courting of Dinah Shadd," etc., etc. | and | THE BOTTLE IMP | BY | ROBERT LOUIS STEVENSON. | New York: M. J. Ivers & Co., Publishers, | 379, Pearl Street. Crown 8vo., pp. iv., numbered, and 116 (excluding "The Bottle Imp," 117—160). Paper wrapper, with design on side, printed in light and dark blue.

The above appeared originally in "The Detroit Free Press," January 3rd to March 28th, 1891.

An Edition, with Introduction, published by Brown and Company, 378 Boylston Street, Boston, 1899. 12mo., pp. 137, Blue cloth, design on side, with Portrait.

LETTERS OF MARQUE. | BY | RUDYARD KIPLING, | Author of | "Plain Tales from the Hills," "Departmental Ditties," etc., etc. | A. H. Wheeler & Co. | Allahabad, | 1891. | [All Rights Reserved.] 12mo., iv. pp. advertisements, pp. vi. (second page of contents numbered ii.), 154, on verso of last page, "Allahabad; | Printed at the 'Pioneer' Press." and advertisements iv. pp. unnumbered. Red and Blue cloth, separated diagonally, lettered | Letters of | Marque | by Rudyard Kipling. This work has been suppressed by Mr. Kipling.

THE | LIGHT THAT FAILED | BY | RUDYARD KIPLING | London | Macmillan and Co. | and New York | 1891 | *All rights reserved.* Crown 8vo., pp. viii., unnumbered, and 339. At the foot of page 339, "*Printed by* R. & R. Clark, *Edinburgh.*" Verso blank. Blue cloth. "Preface: This is the story of *The Light that Failed* | as it was originally conceived by the Writer. | Rudyard Kipling."

This story first appeared in Lippincott's Magazine, Jan., 1891. Pp. 1 to 97, with portrait.

LIFE'S HANDICAP | BEING STORIES OF | MINE OWN PEOPLE. | BY | RUDYARD KIPLING. | I met a hundred men on the road to Delhi and they were all my brothers | Native Proverb. | London | Macmillan & Co. | and New York. N.D. [1891]. Crown 8vo., pp. xiii. and 351. L'Envoi on verso of last page, unnumbered. Blue cloth, gilt top. Contents: "The Incarnation of Krishna Mulvaney," "The Courting of Dinah Shadd," "On Greenhow Hill," "The Man Who Was," "The Head of the District," "Without Benefit of Clergy," "At the End of the Passage," "The Mutiny of the Mavericks," "The Mark of the Beast," "The Return of Imray," "Namgay Doola," "The Lang Men o' Larut," "Bertran and Bimi," "Reingelder and the German Flag," "The Wandering Jew," "Through the Fire," "The Finances of the Gods," "The Amir's Homily," "Jews of Shushan," "The Limitations of Pambé Serang," "Little Tobrah," "Moti Guj—Mutineer," "Bubbling Well Road," "The City of Dreadful Night," "Georgie Porgie," "Naboth," "The Dream of Duncan Parennes."

1892.

THE NAULAHKA: | A STORY OF | WEST AND | EAST | BY RUDYARD KIPLING | and WOLCOT-BALESTIER | London: William Heinemann | MDCCCXCII., Bedford Street, W.C. Crown 8vo., pp. vi., unnumbered, and 276, at the foot of page 276, Printed by Ballantyne Hanson & Co., Edinburgh. Cloth.

A New Edition was published the same year by Macmillan & Co.

BARRACK-ROOM | BALLADS | AND OTHER VERSES BY | RUDYARD KIPLING | (vignette) Methuen and Co. | 18, Bury Street, W.C., | London. 1892. Crown 8vo., pp. xx., numbered, and 208. At foot of page 208, "Printed by T. and A. Constable, Printers to Her Majesty, At the Edinburgh University Press. Many of these poems appeared in the "National Observer," Macmillan's Magazine, "St. James' Gazette," and "The Athenæum." The others were new.

Japanese vellum edition, pp. 208. Bound ¼ parchment, white buckram sides.

1893.

MANY INVENTIONS | BY | RUDYARD KIPLING | "Lo this only have I found, that God hath made man upright; but | they have sought out many inventions."—Ecclesiastes vii., 29. | London | Macmillan & Co. | and New York | 1893. Crown 8vo., pp. x. and 365, on verso of last page, "Printed by R. & R. Clark, Edinburgh." Blue cloth. Contents: "The Disturber of Traffic," "A Conference of the Powers," "My Lord the Elephant," "One View of the Question," "'The Finest Story in the World,'" "His Private Honour," "A Matter of Fact," "The Lost Legion," "In the Rukh," "'Brugglesmith,'" "'Love o' Women,'" "The Record of Badalia Herodsfoot," "Judson and the Empire," "The Children of the Zodiac." "The Record of Badalia Herodsfoot" originally appeared in the Christmas number of "The Detroit Free Press" for 1890. Illustrated.

1894.

MY FIRST BOOK. THE EXPERIENCES OF WALTER BESANT, JAMES PAYN, W. CLARK RUSSELL, GRANT ALLEN, HALL CAINE, G. R. SIMS, RUDYARD KIPLING, etc. London: Chatto & Windus. Kipling's Contribution, pp. 91—97. Large crown 8vo., cloth.

THE | JUNGLE BOOK | BY | RUDYARD KIPLING | With Illustrations | by | J. L. KIPLING, W. H. DRAKE, and P. FRENZENY | London | Macmillan & Co. | and New York | 1894. Crown 8vo., pp. viii., numbered, and 212. At foot of page 212, "*Printed by* R. & R. Clark, *Edinburgh.*" Blue cloth, with design in gold on side and back, gilt edges. Contents: "Mowgli's Brothers," "Hunting-Song of the Seeonee Pack," "Kaa's Hunting," "Road-Song of the Bandar-Log," "'Tiger-Tiger!'" "Mowgli's Song," "The White Seal," "Lukannon," "'Rikki-Tikki-Tavi,'" "Darzee's Chaunt," "Toomai of the Elephants," "Shiv and the Grasshopper," "Servants of the Queen," Parade-Song of the Camp-Animals.

1895.

THE | SECOND JUNGLE BOOK | BY RUDYARD KIPLING. (Vignette) | With Illustrations by | J. LOCKWOOD KIPLING, C.I.E. | London | Macmillan & Co. | and New York | 1895 | *All rights reserved.* Crown 8vo., pp. vi., unnumbered, and 238. At foot of page 238, "Printed by R. & R. Clark, Limited, Edinburgh," In blue cloth. Design of front and back in gold, gilt edges. Contents: "How Fear Came," "The Law of the Jungle," "The Miracle of Purun Bhagat," "A Song of Kahir," "Letting in the Jungle," "Mowgli's Song against People," "The Undertakers," "A Ripple Song," The King's Ankus. "The Song of the Little Hunter," "Quiquern," "Angutivun Tina," "Red Dog," "Chil's Song," "The Spring Running," "The Outsong."

SOLDIERS THREE, | THE STORY OF THE GADSBYS, | IN BLACK AND WHITE. | By | RUDYARD KIPLING. | London | Macmillan & Co., | and New York | 1895 | *All rights reserved.* Crown 8vo., pp. viii., numbered, and 338. At foot of page 338, "*Printed by* R. & R. Clark, *Edinburgh.*" Blue cloth. L'Envoi to "The Story of the Gadsbys" included in index. Crimson cloth, design on side.

"GOOD HUNTING" | BY | RUDYARD KIPLING | [Copyright (1895) *in the United States of America* by Rudyard

Kipling]. "Pall Mall Gazette" Office | 18, Charing Cross Road, London, W.C. | 1895. Medium 8vo. Pp. 16. At foot of page 16, "Printed for the Proprietors of the PALL MALL GAZETTE by THOMAS HUNT, at the Office, 18, Charing Cross Road, in the Parish of St. Martin's-in-the-Fields, Middlesex.' Paper wrapper.

OUT OF INDIA | THINGS I SAW, AND FAILED TO SEE, IN | CERTAIN DAYS AND NIGHTS AT | JEYPORE AND ELSEWHERE | BY | RUDYARD KIPLING | New York: | Copyright, 1895, By | G. W. Dillingham, Publisher, | Successor to G. W. Carleton & Co. | MDCCCXCV. | [*All Rights Reserved.*] N. D. Crown 8vo., pp. vi. (numbered), and 340. Pale blue linen, with a design on front and back.

TOMMY | AND OTHER POEMS | FOR RECITATION | RUDYARD KIPLING | Lewis Carroll Norman Gale | May Kendall Hal Findon | Constance E. Naden | Mary E. Manners | "P" | London | James Clarke & Co., 13 & 14, Fleet Street. | 1895. | Pp. x., numbered, and 98; in centre of blank page facing last, "London: W. Speaight and Sons, Printers, Fetter Lane." Fcap. 8vo., limp cloth wrappers, with design on front.

The above volume contains one only of Kipling's poems, the one from which the volume takes its title.

1896.

THE SEVEN SEAS. | BY RUDYARD KIPLING. | (Vignette) Methuen & Co. | 36, Essex Street, W.C. | London. | 1896. Crown 8vo., pp. xviii., numbered, and 230. At the foot of page 230, "Printed by T. & A. Constable, Printers to Her Majesty, at the Edinburgh University Press." Marone buckram, lettered on back.

There was also a large paper edition.

SOLDIER TALES. | BY | RUDYARD KIPLING. | London. | Macmillan & Co., Ltd. | New York : The Macmillan Co. | 1896 | *All rights reserved.* Post 8vo., pp. viii., numbered, and 172. Blue cloth, gilt edges. Illustrated by A. S. Hartrick. All the stories in this volume had appeared before in "Wee Willie Winkie," "Life's Handicap," "Plain Tales," etc. Contents : "With the Main Guard," "The Drums of the Fore and Aft," "The Man Who Was," "The Courting of Dinah Shadd," "The Incarnation of Krishna Mulvaney," "The Taking of Lungtungpen," "The Madness of Private Ortheris."

1897.

AN ALMANAC OF TWELVE SPORTS FOR 1898. By William Nicholson. Twelve Coloured Plates, each illustrating a sport for the month. With accompanying Rhymes by Rudyard Kipling. 4to. In three editions.

WHITE HORSES | BY | RUDYARD KIPLING | London | Printed for Private Circulation | 1897. Globe 8vo., pp. 10. Blue paper wrapper, with repetition of title page.

'CAPTAINS COURAGEOUS.' | A STORY OF THE GRAND BANKS. | BY | RUDYARD KIPLING. | With illustrations by | I. W. Taber. | London : | Macmillan and Co , Limited. | New York : The Macmillan Company, | 1897. | *All rights reserved.* Crown 8vo., pp. viii., numbered, and 245. At bottom of page 245, "*Printed by* R. & R. Clark, *Limited, Edinburgh.*" Verso blank. With 22 illustrations. Blue cloth, lettered on side, with a design in gold, gilt edges.

1898.

THE DAY'S WORK. | BY | RUDYARD KIPLING. | London | Macmillan & Co. | 1898 | *All rights reserved.* Crown 8vo., pp. vi., unnumbered, and 381. At the foot of page

381, *Printed by* R. & R. Clark. Limited, *Edinburgh.* Verso blank. Blue cloth. Contents: "The Bridge-Builders," "A Walking Delegate," "The Ship that Found Herself," "The Tomb of His Ancestors," "The Devil and the Deep Sea," "William the Conqueror," Part I., "William the Conqueror," Part II., "·007," "The Maltese Cat," "'Bread Upon the Waters,'" "An Error of the Fourth Dimension," "My Sunday at Home," "The Brushwood Boy."

The American Edition of the above is illustrated with a cover designed by the author. Ex. crown 8vo., pp. xiv. and 431, verso of last page blank.

A FLEET IN BEING. | NOTES OF TWO TRIPS WITH THE | CHANNEL SQUADRON. | BY | RUDYARD KIPLING. | London. | Macmillan and Co., Limited | New York: | The Macmillan Company | 1898 | All rights reserved. Originally published in the "Morning Post," Nov. 5 to 11, 1898. Crown 8vo. pp. iv., unnumbered, and 84. At foot of page 84, Richard Clay and Sons, Limited, London and Bungay. Two Editions, in blue cloth and blue paper wrapper respectively, with design on side.

COLLECTANEA | Being certain reprinted | verses as written | by RUDYARD KIPLING | the Explanation | the Vampire | Mandalay | Recessional | the Three Captains | Set into type and imprinted for | M. F. Mansfield, New York | MDCCCXCVIII. | Small 8vo., pp. 32. Grey paper boards.

1899.

FROM SEA TO SEA | LETTERS OF TRAVEL | BY RUDYARD KIPLING | [Publisher's device]. Volume I | [II]. "Write me as one that loved his fellow-men" | New York | Doubleday & McClure Company | 1899 | Crown 8vo. Bound in green cloth, cut edges, green tops, enclosed in wrappers and a cardboard box. Vol. I., pp. xiv., 460. Vol. II., pp. x.,

o. Contents:—Vol. I. Letters of Marque; From Sea to Sea. Vol. II. From Sea to Sea; City of Dreadful Night; Among the Railway Folk; The Giridih Coal-Fields; In an Opium Factory; The Smith Administration.

STALKY & CO. | By | RUDYARD KIPLING. | London | Macmillan & Co., Limited | 1899 | *All rights reserved.* Lg. crown 8vo., pp. x., numbered, and 272. At foot of page 272: "Printed by R. & R. Clark, Limited, Edinburgh." Dedication: "To | Cornell Price | Headmaster, United Services College | Westward Ho! Bideford, North Devon | 1874—1894." Bound in red cloth, as Uniform Edition. Introductory Poem, pp. vii.—ix. Contents: "In Ambush," "Slaves of the Lamp, Part I.," "An Unsavoury Interlude," "The Impressionists," "The Moral Reformers," "A Little Peep," "The Flag of their Country," "The Last Term," "Slaves of the Lamp, Part II." Reprinted from "Cosmopolis," "Pearson's Magazine," and "The Windsor Magazine."

BOOKS RELATING TO RUDYARD KIPLING.

THE KIPLING | BIRTHDAY BOOK | COMPILED BY | JOSEPH FINN | (Authorised by RUDYARD KIPLING) | You may twist it, you may turn it, you may prose it till | you drop, But the way to Pilly-Winky's not the way to Winky-Pop! | *Jungle Book* | London | Macmillan and Co., Ltd. | New York: The Macmillan Co. | 1896. Demy 16mo., pp. iv., unnumbered, and 278. In centre of blank page facing p. 278, "Printed by R. & R. Clark, Limited, *Edinburgh*." With illustrations by J. Lockwood Kipling. Light green linen, with design, which is repeated on end-papers.

THE COURTING OF DINAH SHADD. A | CONTRIBUTION TO A BIBLIOGRAPHY OF | THE WRITINGS OF RUDYARD KIPLING. | N.D. [1898]. Square 16mo., pp. 21. On last page, "One hundred and twenty copies of this Contribution to a Bibliography of the Writings of Rudyard Kipling were printed for Subscribers on the Marion Press,. Jamaica, Queensborough, New York, in the month of March, Eighteen Hundred and Ninety-Eight. This copy is No. . . . Printed for . . . French grey wrappers.

THE RELIGION OF | MR. KIPLING. | By | W. B. PARKER. | M. F. Mansfield and A. Wessels, | New York 1899. Pott 8vo., pp. 22. Paper boards.

THRO' THE YEAR WITH | KIPLING | Being a Year-Book of Selections from the Earlier | Works of Mr. Rudyard Kipling | with Introduction and Bibliography | "It's all in the day's work." | Kipling: "Thrown Away." | Boston | Brown and Company, MDCCCXCIX. Fcap. 8vo., pp. vi., numbered, and 144. Green cloth design on side. With Portrait.

A KEN OF KIPLING | Being | a Biographical Sketch of | Rudyard Kipling, with an | Appreciation and some | Anecdotes. | By | WILL M. CLEMENS | Author of | "Theodore Roosevelt the American," "The Life of Mark | Twain," "The Depew Story Book," etc., etc. | (Design). | New Amsterdam Book Company | 156, Fifth Avenue, New York | MDCCCXCIX. Small crown 8vo., 141 pp. Bound in orange linen, design on side. With Portrait.

A KIPLING NOTE BOOK | Illustrations, Anecdotes, Biblio | graphical and Biographical Facts | anent this Foremost Writer of | Fiction. | Published by | M. F. Mansfield and A. Wessels, 1135, Broadway, New York. No. I. published February, 1899, and monthly since that date.

THE BUDGET. | A reprint of the issues of May 14th | and May 28th, 1898; containing | contributions | by RUDYARD KIPLING | and | MAX BEERBOHM. Printed for and published by | M.F.Mansfield and A.Wessels | New York, MDCCCXCIX. Pott 8vo., pp. 32. Paper boards.

RUDYARD KIPLING. | An Attempt at Appreciation | By | G. F. MONKSHOOD. | (W. J. Clarke). | London. | Greening & Co. | 20 Cecil Court, Charing Cross Road, W.C. | 1899. | All Rights Reserved. Crown 8vo., pp. x. numbered, and 236. "The Envoy" facing last page, unnumbered, advertisement on verso. With Portrait, bound in marone buckram.

UNIFORM EDITIONS OF THE WORKS OF RUDYARD KIPLING

1897-8.

THE NOVELS, TALES, AND POEMS OF RUDYARD KIPLING (Edition de Luxe).

Volume I. Plain Tales from the Hills. Sept., 1897.
,, II. Soldiers Three and Military Tales. I. Oct., 1897.
,, III. ,, ,, ,, II. Nov., 1897.
,, IV. In Black and White. Dec., 1897.
,, V. The Phantom 'Rickshaw, and Other Stories. Jan., 1898.
,, VI. Under the Deodars, Story of the Gadsbys, and Wee Willie Winkie. Feb., 1898.
,, VII. The Jungle Book. March, 1898.
,, VIII. The Second Jungle Book. April, 1898.
,, IX. The Light that Failed. May, 1898.
,, X. The Naulahka. June, 1898.
,, XI. Poems. July, 1898.
,, XII. Captains Courageous. August, 1898.

This edition was limited to 1050 copies, and was published by Macmillan & Co. A new portrait (from life) was etched by Mr. William Strang for this work. A uniform edition of "Departmental Ditties" was published by Thacker & Co., also limited to 1050 copies.

1897-8.

"THE OUTWARD BOUND EDITION" OF RUDYARD KIPLING'S WORKS (American).

Volume I. Plain Tales from the Hills.
,, II. Soldiers Three and Military Tales. I.
,, III. ,, ,, ,, II.
,, IV. In Black and White.
,, V. The Phantom 'Rickshaw, and other Stories.
,, VI. Under the Deodars, Story of the Gadsbys, and Wee Willie Winkie.
,, VII. The Jungle Book.
,, VIII. The Second Jungle Book.
,, IX. The Light that Failed.
,, X. The Naulahka.
,, XI. Poems.
,, XII. Captains Courageous.

In Preparation.

,, XIII. The Day's Work. Part I., including The Son of His Father.
,, XIV. The Day's Work. Part II., with the addition of several Stories not included under that title in other editions.
,, XV. and XVI. From Sea to Sea.
,, XVII. Early Verse, including School-Boy Lyrics, Echoes, and Departmental Ditties.
,, XVIII. Stalky & Co.

Large crown 8vo., bound in marone cloth, with cameo of an elephant's head on side. Charles Scribner and Sons, New York.

1899.

NEW EDITION OF THE PROSE WRITINGS OF RUDYARD KIPLING.

Volume I. Plain Tales from the Hills.

,, II. Life's Handicap. Being Stories of Mine Own People.

,, III. Many Inventions.

,, IV. The Light that Failed. Re-written and considerably enlarged.

,, V. Wee Willie Winkie, and other Stories.

,, VI. Soldiers Three, and other Stories.

,, VII. The Jungle Book. With Illustrations by J. L. Kipling and W. H. Drake.

,, VIII. The Second Jungle Book. With Illustrations by J. Lockwood Kipling.

,, IX. Captains Courageous: a Story of the Grand Banks With Illustrations by I. W. Taber.

,, X. The Day's Work.

,, XI. Stalky & Co.

In course of publication.

Large Crown 8vo. Red cloth, gilt tops. With cameo in gold on side. Macmillan and Co.

SHORT PIECES IN PROSE AND VERSE BY RUDYARD KIPLING,

Not yet published in book form.

PROSE.

"Genuine." *The Week's News*, Allahabad, January 7th, 1888.

"The Likes o' Us." *The Week's News*, Allahabad, February 4th, 1888.

"His Brother's Keeper." *The Week's News*, Allahabad, April 7th, 1888.

"'Sleipner,' late 'Thurinda.'" *The Week's News*, Allahabad, May 12th, 1888.

"A Supplementary Chapter." *The Week's News*, Allahabad, May 19th, 1888.

"The Peculiar Embarrassment of Justus Krenk." *The Week's News*, July 28th, 1888.

"The Last of the Stories." *The Week's News*, Allahabad, September 15th, 1888.

"The Wandering Jew," "Abaft the Funnel" (Nos. II., III., and IV.), "It." *Turnovers*, Vol. VI., April to June, 1889. Published by *The Civil and Military Gazette*, Lahore.

"Abaft the Funnel" (Nos VI. and VII.), "The Red Lamp," "Griffiths," "The Safe Man," "The Shadow of His Hand," "Abaft the Funnel" (No. VIII.), "The Bow Hume Cable Car," "A Little More Beef," "Her Little Responsibilities." *Turnovers*, Vol. VII., July to September, 1889. Published by *The Civil and Military Gazette*, Lahore.

"The History of a Fall," "The New Dispensation" (I. and II). *Turnovers*, Vol. VIII., September to December, 1889. Published by *The Civil and Military Gazette*, Lahore.

"The Three Young Men. *London in a Fog*," "My Great and Only," "The Betrayal of Confidences," "The Adoration of the Magi," "A Death in the Camp," "A Really Good Time," "On Exhibition." *Turnovers*, Vol. IX., January to March, 1890. Published by *The Civil and Military Gazette*, Lahore.

"One View of the Question." *The Fortnightly Review*, February, 1890.

"'For One Night Only.'" *Longman's Magazine*, April, 1890.

"The Lamentable Comedy of Willow Wood." *The Fortnightly Review*, May, 1890.|

"The Enlightenments of Pagett, M.P." *Contemporary Review*, September, 1890.

"Mrs. Hauksbee Sits Out": An Historical Extravaganza (Illustrated). *Illustrated London News Christmas Number*, 1890.

A Letter "To Certain Odd Volumes." Printed in *The Year-Boke of the Sette of Odd Volnmes*, No. 3, 1890–1. Pp. 50 51. Privately printed.

"The Last Relief" (Illustrated). *The Ludgate*, May, 1891.

"The Edge of the East." Part I. *The Civil and Military Gazette*, Lahore, July 9, 1892.

———————— Part II. *Ibid.*, July 16, 1892.

"'Our Overseas Men.'" Part I. *The Civil and Military Gazette*, Lahore, August 8, 1892.

——————— Part II. *Ibid.*, August 15, 1892.

"'Some Earthquakes.'" Part I. *The Civil and Military Gazette*, Lahore, August 22, 1892.

——————— Part II. *Ibid.*, August 27, 1892.

"'Half-a-Dozen Pictures.'" I. *The Civil and Military Gazette*, Lahore, September 3, 1892.

——————— II. *Ibid.*, September 5, 1892.

"The Legs of Sister Ursula" (Illustrated). *The Idler*, June, 1893.

"Mother of Mine." *To-Day*, June 2nd, 1894.

"Winning the Victoria Cross." (Illustrated). *The Windsor Magazine*, June, 1897.

"Pharaoh and the Sergeant." *McClure's Magazine*, September, 1897.

"The Feet of the Young Men." *Scribner's Magazine*, December, 1897.

"A Letter to "The Budget." A Magazine published by the boys at Horsmonden School. No. 14, May 28th, 1898.

"Landscape and Literature." A Letter to the *Spectator*, July 2nd, 1898.

"The Burning of the *Sarah Sands*" (Illustrated). *Black and White Christmas Number*, 1898.

"Literary Property. I.—Kipling *v.* Putnam." Mr. Rudyard Kipling's Statement. *The Author*, London, July 1, 1899.

VERSE.

"In Partibus." *Turnovers*, Vol. VIII., October to December, 1889. Published by *The Civil and Military Gazette*, Lahore.

"Some Notes on a Bill." *The Author*, London, July, 1891.

"The Exile's Line." *The Civil and Military Gazette*, Lahore, July 8, 1892.

"The Gipsy Trail." *The Century Magazine*, December, 1892.

"Primum Tempus." *The Idler*, December, 1892.

Introductory Verses to "Steve Brown's Bunyip, and other Stories." By J. A. Barry. Remington & Co., Limited, London and Sydney, 1893.

"'Bobs'" (Illustrated). *The Pall Mall Magazine*, December, 1893.

"An Unqualified Pilot" (Illustrated). *The Windsor Magazine*, February, 1895.

"Our Lady of the Snows." *Times*, April 27, 1897.

"The Vampire." Catalogue, Tenth Summer Exhibition, New Gallery, 1897. Written for Mr. (now Sir) Philip Burne Jones's picture of that name.

"Recessional." *The Times*, July 17, 1897. Reprinted in *Literature*, November 27, 1897, and April 29, 1899.

"White Horses." *Literature*, October 23rd, 1897.

"The Destroyers" (Illustrated). *The Windsor Magazine*, June, 1898.

'The Truce of the Bear." *Literature*, October 1, 1898.

"Kitchener's School." *The Times*, December 8, 1898. Reprinted in *Literature*, December 10, 1898.

"The White Man's Burden." *Times* and *Literature*, February 4th, and *McClure's Magazine*, February, 1899.

"Cruisers." *The Morning Post*, August 14, 1899.

"The Old Issue." *Times*, September 29th, 1899.

An Index to Short Stories by Rudyard Kipling that have been published in book form.

Title of Story.	Title of Book.
Amir's Homily (The).	*Life's Handicap.*
Among the Railway Folk.	*The City of Dreadful Night.*
———	*From Sea to Sea, Vol. II.*
Arrest of Lieut. Golightly (The).	*Plain Tales.*
At the End of the Passage.	*Life's Handicap.*
At Howli Thana.	*In Black and White.*
At the Pit's Mouth.	*Under the Deodars.*
At Twenty-Two.	*In Black and White.*
Baa Baa Black Sheep.	*Wee Willie Winkie.*
Bank Fraud (A).	*Plain Tales.*
Bisara of Pooree (The).	*Plain Tales.*
Bertran and Bimi.	*Life's Handicap.*
Beyond the Pale.	*Plain Tales.*
Big Drunk Draf' (The).	*Soldiers Three.*

TITLE OF STORY.	TITLE OF BOOK.
Black Jack.	*Soldiers Three.*
'Bread Upon the Waters.'	*The Day's Work.*
Bridge-Builders (The).	*The Day's Work.*
Broken - link Handicap (The).	*Plain Tales.*
Bronckhorst Divorce-Case (The).	*Plain Tales.*
'Brugglesmith.'	*Many Inventions.*
Brushwood Boy (The).	*The Day's Work.*
Bubbling Well Road.	*Life's Handicap.*
By Word of Mouth.	*Plain Tales.*
Children of the Zodiac (The).	*Many Inventions.*
City of Dreadful Night (The).	*The City of Dreadful Night.*
———	*Life's Handicap.*
———	*From Sea to Sea, Vol. II.*
Conference of the Powers (A).	*Many Inventions.*
Consequences.	*Plain Tales.*
Conversion of Aurelian McGoggin (The).	*Plain Tales.*
Courting of Dinah Shadd (The).	*Life's Handicap.*
———	*Soldier Tales.*
Cupid's Arrows.	*Plain Tales.*
Daughter of the Regiment (The).	*Plain Tales.*

Title of Story.	Title of Book.
Devil and the Deep Sea (The).	*The Day's Work.*
Disturber of Traffic (The).	*Many Inventions.*
Dray Wara Yow Dee.	*In Black and White.*
Dream of Duncan Parrenness (The).	*Life's Handicap.*
Drums of the Fore and Aft (The).	*Wee Willie Winkie.*
———	*Soldier Tales.*
Education of Otis Yeere (The).	*Under the Deodars.*
Error of the Fourth Dimension (An).	*The Day's Work.*
False Dawn.	*Plain Tales.*
Fatima.	*Story of the Gadsbys.*
Finances of the Gods (The).	*Life's Handicap.*
'Finest Story in the World' (The).	*Many Inventions.*
Flag of their Country (The).	*Stalky and Co.*
Friend's Friend (A).	*Plain Tales.*
From Sea to Sea.	*From Sea to Sea, Vol. I.*
———	*From Sea to Sea, Vol. II.*
Garden of Eden (The).	*Story of Gadsbys.*
Gate of the Hundred Sorrows (The).	*Plain Tales.*
Gemini.	*In Black and White.*
Georgie Porgee.	*Life's Handicap.*

Title of Story.	Title of Book.
Germ Destroyer (A).	*Plain Tales.*
———	*Soldier Tales.*
Giridih Coal Fields (The).	*The City of Dreadful Night.*
———	*From Sea to Sea, Vol. II.*
God from the Machine (The).	*Soldiers Three.*
Head of the District (The).	*Life's Handicap.*
Hill of Illusion (The).	*Under the Deodars.*
His Chance in Life.	*Plain Tales.*
His Majesty the King.	*Wee Willie Winkie.*
His Private Honour.	*Many Inventions.*
His Wedded Wife.	*Plain Tales.*
How Fear Came.	*Second Jungle Book.*
Impressionists (The).	*Stalky and Co.*
In an Opium Factory.	*The City of Dreadful Night.*
Incarnation of Krishna Mulvaney (The).	*Life's Handicap.*
———	*Soldier Tales.*
———	*From Sea to Sea, Vol. II.*
In Error.	*Plain Tales.*
In Flood Time.	*In Black and White.*
In the House of Suddhoo.	*Plain Tales.*
In the Matter of a Private.	*Soldiers Three.*
In the Pride of his Youth.	*Plain Tales.*
In the Rukh.	*Many Inventions.*
Jews in Shushan.	*Life's Handicap.*

Title of Story.	Title of Book.
Judgment of Dungara (The).	*In Black and White.*
Judson and the Empire.	*Many Inventions.*
Kaa's Hunting.	*Jungle Book.*
Kidnapped.	*Plain Tales.*
King's Ankus (The).	*Second Jungle Book.*
Lang Men o' Larut (The).	*Life's Handicap.*
Last Term (The).	*Stalky and Co.*
Letters of Marque.	*From Sea to Sea, Vol. I.*
Letting in the Jungle.	*Second Jungle Book.*
Limitations of Pambé Serang (The).	*Life's Handicap.*
Lispeth.	*Plain Tales.*
Little Peep (A).	*Stalky and Co.*
Little Tobrah.	*Life's Handicap.*
Lost Legion (The).	*Many Inventions.*
'Love o' Women.'	*Many Inventions.*
Maltese Cat (The).	*The Day's Work.*
Madness of Private Ortheris (The).	*Soldier Tales.*
———	*Plain Tales.*
Man Who Was (The).	*Life's Handicap.*
———	*Soldier Tales.*
Man Who Would be King (The).	*The Phantom 'Rickshaw.*
Mark of the Beast (The).	*Life's Handicap.*
Matter of Fact (A).	*Many Inventions.*

TITLE OF STORY.	TITLE OF BOOK.
Miracle of Purun Bhagat (The).	*Second Jungle Book.*
Miss Youghal's Sais.	*Plain Tales.*
Moral Reformers (The).	*Stalky and Co.*
Moti Guj—Mutineer.	*Life's Handicap.*
Mowgli's Brothers.	*Jungle Book.*
Mutiny of the Mavericks (The).	*Life's Handicap.*
My Lord the Elephant.	*Many Inventions.*
My Own True Ghost Story.	*The Phantom 'Rickshaw.*
My Sunday at Home.	*The Day's Work.*
Naboth.	*Life's Handicap.*
Namgay Doola.	*Life's Handicap.*
·007.	*The Day's Work.*
On the City Wall.	*In Black aud White.*
On Greenhow Hill.	*Life's Handicap.*
Only a Subaltern.	*Under the Deodars.*
On the Strength of a Likeness.	*Plain Tales.*
One View of the Question.	*Many Inventions.*
Other Man (The).	*Plain Tales.*
Phantom 'Rickshaw (The).	*The Phantom 'Rickshaw.*
———	*Quartette.*
'Pig.'	*Plain Tales.*
Poor Dear Mamma.	*Story of Gadsbys.*

TITLE OF STORY.	TITLE OF BOOK.
Private Learoyd's Story.	*Soldiers Three.*
Quiquern.	*Second Jungle Book.*
Red Dog.	*Second Jungle Book.*
Record of Badalia Herodsfoot (The).	*Many Inventions.*
Reingelder and the German Flag.	*Life's Handicap.*
Rescue of Pluffles (The).	*Plain Tales.*
Return of Imray (The).	*Life's Handicap.*
'Rikki-Tikki-Tavi.'	*Jungle Book.*
Rout of White Hussars (The).	*Plain Tales.*
Second-Rate Woman (A).	*Under the Deodars.*
Sending of Dana Da (The).	*In Black and White.*
Servants of the Queen.	*Jungle Book.*
Ship that Found Herself (The).	*The Day's Work.*
Slaves of the Lamp. Parts I. and II.	*Stalky and Co.*
Smith Administration (The).	*From Sea to Sea, Vol. II.*
Solid Muldoon (The).	*Soldiers Three.*
Spring Running (The).	*Second Jungle Book.*
Story of Muhammad Din (The).	*Plain Tales.*
Strange Ride of Morrowbie Jukes (The).	*Quartette.*

Title of Story.	Title of Book.
Strange Ride of Morrowble Jukes (The).	*The Phantom 'Rickshaw.*
Swelling of Jordan (The).	*Story of Gadsbys.*
Taking of Lungtungpen (The).	*Soldiers Three.*
———	*Plain Tales.*
———	*Soldier Tales.*
Tents of Kedar (The).	*Story of Gadsbys.*
Three and—an Extra.	*Plain Tales.*
Three Musketeers (The).	*Plain Tales.*
Through the Fire.	*Life's Handicap.*
Thrown Away.	*Plain Tales.*
'Tiger-Tiger.'	*Jungle Book.*
Tods' Amendment.	*Plain Tales.*
Tomb of His Ancestors (The).	*The Day's Work.*
To be Filed for Reference.	*Plain Tales.*
Toomai of the Elephants.	*Jungle Book.*
Undertakers (The).	*Second Jungle Book.*
Unsavoury Interlude (An).	*Stalky and Co.*
Valley of the Shadow (The).	*Story of Gadsbys.*
Venus Annodomini.	*Plain Tales.*
Walking Delegate (A).	*The Day's Work.*
Wandering Jew (The).	*Life's Handicap.*
Watches of the Night.	*Plain Tales.*
Wayside Comedy (A).	*Under the Deodars.*
Wee Willie Winkie.	*Wee Willie Winkie.*

Title of Story.	Title of Book.
White Seal (The).	*Jungle Book.*
With the Main Guard.	*Soldiers Three.*
———	*Soldier Tales.*
William the Conqueror, Parts I. and II.	*The Day's Work.*
With any Amazement.	*Story of Gadsbys.*
Without Benefit of Clergy.	*Life's Handicap.*
World Without (The).	*Story of Gadsbys.*
Wressley of the Foreign Office.	*Plain Tales.*
'Yoked with an Unbeliever.'	*Plain Tales.*

An Index to Poems by Rudyard Kipling that have been published in book form.

Abbreviations: The Seven Seas, "S.S." Barrack Room Ballads, "B.R.B." Departmental Ditties, "D.D." The Jungle Book, "J.B." The Second Jungle Book, "2nd J.B."

Title of Poem.	Title of Book.
Man Who Could Write.	*D.D.* 32.
Mare's Nest (The).	*D.D.* 84.
Mary Gloster (The).	*S.S.* 142.
'Mary, Pity Women!'	*S.S.* 222.
Masque of Plenty (The).	*D.D.* 75.
'Men that Fought at Minden (The).'	*S.S.* 182.
Merchantmen (The).	*S.S.* 26.
Miracles (The).	*S.S.* 47.
Moon of Other Days (The).	*D.D.* 137.
Mother-Lodge (The).	*S.S.* 196.
Mowgli's Song.	*J.B.*
Mowgli's Song against People.	2*nd J.B.*
Mulholland's Contract.	*S.S.* 88.
Municipal.	*D.D.* 38.
My Rival.	*D.D.* 45.
Native-Born (The).	*S.S.* 49.
Old Song (An).	*D.D.* 127.
One Viceroy Resigns.	*D.D.* 148.
Oonts.	*B.R.B.* 27.
Outsong (The).	2*nd J.B.*
Overland Mail (The).	*D.D.* 69.
Pagett, M.P.	*D.D.* 54.
Parade-Song of the Camp-Animals.	*J.B.*
Pink Dominoes.	*D.D.* 35.

Title of Poem.	Title of Book.
Song of Kahir (A).	*2nd J.B.*
Song of the Banjo (The).	*S.S.* 78.
Song of the Cities (The).	*S.S.* 11.
Song of the Dead (The).	*S.S.* 5.
Song of the English (A).	*S.S.* 1.
Song of the Little Hunter (The)	*2nd J.B.*
Song of the Sons (The).	*S.S.* 10.
Song of the Women (The).	*D.D.* 10.
Story of Ung (The).	*S.S.* 128.
Story of Uriah (The).	*D.D.* 16.
Study of an Elevation, in Indian Ink.	*D.D.* 6.
Tale of Two Cities (A).	*D.D.* 164.
That Day.	*S.S.* 179.
Three-Decker (The).	*S.S.* 134.
Tomlinson.	*B.R.B.* 192.
Tommy.	*B.R.B.* 6.
To the True Romance.	*S.S.* 106.
To the Unknown Goddess.	*D.D.* 49.
Troopin'.	*B.R.B.* 54.
Two Months.	*D.D.* 175.
Undertaker's Horse (The).	*D.D.* 145.
What Happened.	*D.D.* 28.
What the People Said.	*D.D.* 142.
Widow at Windsor (The).	*B.R.B.* 39.
Widow's Party (The).	*B.R.B.* 57.
With Scindia to Delhi.	*B.R.B.* 103.
Young British Soldier (The).	*B.R.B.* 46.